T0323604

Cambridge Elements ≡

Elements in England in the Early Medieval World
edited by
Megan Cavell
University of Birmingham
Rory Naismith
University of Cambridge
Winfried Rudolf
University of Göttingen
Emily V. Thornbury
Yale University

ENTERTAINMENT, PLEASURE, AND MEANING IN EARLY ENGLAND

Martha Bayless
University of Oregon

CAMBRIDGE
UNIVERSITY PRESS

Shaftesbury Road, Cambridge CB2 8EA, United Kingdom

One Liberty Plaza, 20th Floor, New York, NY 10006, USA

477 Williamstown Road, Port Melbourne, VIC 3207, Australia

314–321, 3rd Floor, Plot 3, Splendor Forum, Jasola District Centre,
New Delhi – 110025, India

103 Penang Road, #05–06/07, Visioncrest Commercial, Singapore 238467

Cambridge University Press is part of Cambridge University Press & Assessment,
a department of the University of Cambridge.

We share the University's mission to contribute to society through the pursuit of
education, learning and research at the highest international levels of excellence.

www.cambridge.org
Information on this title: www.cambridge.org/9781009517119

DOI: 10.1017/9781009161107

© Martha Bayless 2024

This publication is in copyright. Subject to statutory exception and to the provisions
of relevant collective licensing agreements, no reproduction of any part may take
place without the written permission of Cambridge University Press & Assessment.

When citing this work, please include a reference to the DOI 10.1017/9781009161107

First published 2024

A catalogue record for this publication is available from the British Library.

ISBN 978-1-009-51711-9 Hardback
ISBN 978-1-009-16282-1 Paperback
ISSN 2632-203X (online)
ISSN 2632-2021 (print)

Cambridge University Press & Assessment has no responsibility for the persistence
or accuracy of URLs for external or third-party internet websites referred to in this
publication and does not guarantee that any content on such websites is, or will
remain, accurate or appropriate.

Entertainment, Pleasure, and Meaning in Early England

Elements in England in the Early Medieval World

DOI: 10.1017/9781009161107
First published online: November 2024

Martha Bayless
University of Oregon

Author for correspondence: Martha Bayless, mjbayles@uoregon.edu

Abstract: The people of early England (*c.* 450–1100 CE) enjoyed numerous kinds of entertainment, recreation, and pleasure, but the scattered records of such things have made the larger picture challenging to assemble. This Element illuminates the merrier aspects of early English life, extending our understanding of the full range of early medieval English culture. It shows why entertainment and festivity were not merely trivial aspects of culture, but had important functions – in ritual, in community building, in assuming power, and in resistance to power. Among the activities explored are child's play; drinking and feasting; music, dance, and performance; the pleasures of literature; festivals and celebrations; hunting and sport; and games.

Keywords: Anglo-Saxon, England, culture, performance, entertainment

© Martha Bayless 2024

ISBNs: 9781009517119 (HB), 9781009162821 (PB), 9781009161107 (OC)
ISSNs: 2632-203X (online), 2632-2021 (print)

Contents

1 Introduction: Entertainment in Anglo-Saxon England   1

2 Child's Play   5

3 Drinking and Feasting   11

4 Music, Dance, and Performance   25

5 The Pleasures of Literature   38

6 Festivals and Celebrations   45

7 Hunting and Sport   52

8 Games and Play   60

9 Conclusions: The Silent Hall   70

References   72

1 Introduction: Entertainment in Anglo-Saxon England

> Saturnus cwæð:
> 'Ac forhwan beoð ða gesiðas　　somod
> 　　ætgædre,
> wop and hleahtor? ... '
> Salomon cuæð:
> 'Unlæde bið and ormod　　se ðe a wile
> geomrian on gihðe;　se bið gode fracoðast.'[1]
> (Saturn spoke:
> 'But why are they companions, both together —
>
> weeping and laughter?
> Solomon spoke:
> 'He is wretched and hopeless, the one who
> 　　always wants
> to be miserable in anxiety; he is most offensive
> 　　to God.')
> 　　　　　　　　— *Solomon and Saturn*, 348–49, 351–52

One depiction of merriment may serve as an emblem for the entire project of describing entertainment and play in Anglo-Saxon England. The *Rune Poem* lays out a scene of enjoyment:

> *Peorð* byþ symble　　plega and hlehter
> wlancum ...　　ðar wigan sittaþ
> on beorsele　　bliþe ætsomne.[2]
>
> (*Peorð* is play and laughter to the proud ones at the feast ... where warriors sit together merrily in the beer hall.)

The sources of play and laughter are exactly what this Element is exploring, and *peorð* would therefore seem highly relevant to the enterprise, but the problem is that the meaning of the word *peorð* is completely unknown.[3] The many sources of play and laughter in Anglo-Saxon England are not quite so obscure, but the scattered nature of the records has made the larger picture challenging to assemble. Such an endeavour is nevertheless worthwhile, enriching as it must our understanding of the full range of early medieval English culture: not merely serious, sophisticated, often learned, sometimes warlike and always

---

[1] Dobbie, *Anglo-Saxon Minor Poems*, p. 43. All translations not otherwise attributed are my own; where there is no footnote citation following a translation, this indicates that the translation is mine.

[2] Dobbie, *Anglo-Saxon Minor Poems*, p. 29 (lines 38–40).

[3] Suggestions as to the meaning of *peorð* include 'playing piece for a board game', 'horse', 'throat/gullet', 'apple tree', and 'pear', but no certain conclusion is possible. See, for instance, Dobbie, *Anglo-Saxon Minor Poems*, p. 156; Schneider, *Die germanischen Runennamen*, pp. 411–35; Düwel, *Runenkunde*, pp. 197–202; Mees, 'Batavian *Pero*'.

multifaceted, but also often playful and merry. Entertainment and festivity had important functions in ritual, in community building, in consolidating power, and in resistance to power. The survival of certain types of sources has weighted the importance of church and government to the period, and although entertainment and play were surprisingly common even in those realms, adding in the pastimes and celebrations of ordinary people can give us a multifaceted picture of society, in which the serious and the playful had a complex and interconnected relationship.

The ways in which merriment was manifested in Anglo-Saxon England are in some aspects familiar: drinking and feasting, music, dance, storytelling and poetry, hunting, sport, and games. Although these were woven into everyday life, there were also special occasions more wholly given over to celebration and festivity. Ironically, many glimpses at Anglo-Saxon merriment come from the clerics who complained about them, and in particular complained about those in the religious life who were far too merry for the liking of the more sombre. These descriptions start in the earliest records. The Penitential of Theodore, a Frankish compilation attributed to Theodore, Archbishop of Canterbury (668–690), expressed disapproval about some of the pastimes of the secular clergy:

> Jocationes, et saltationes, et circum, vel cantica turpia et luxuriosa, vel lusa diabolica, nec ad ipsas æcclesias, nec in dominibus, nec in plateis, nec in ullo loco alio facere præsumat; quia hoc de paganorum consuetudine remansit.[4]

> (They should not presume to indulge in merriments, and dances, and races, or shameful and bawdy songs, or devilish playings, neither in churches nor in dwellings nor in the streets nor in any other place; for this remains from the customs of the pagans.)

This was the kind of formulaic set of rules that might be passed down the ages regardless of local conditions, but it is clear that local conditions did involve all of these entertainments. Although culture and traditions naturally varied from place to place and at different dates within the Anglo-Saxon period, similar entertainments – and similar complaints about those entertainments – crop up across the era. The scarcity of surviving records tells us little about very localised practices, but suggests that many forms of entertainment were widely and long-lastingly popular. As early as the eighth century, Bede was complaining about the secular games and sports that accompanied the Days of Rogation, days that were supposed to be set aside for sombre prayer and reflection.[5] Despite Bede, the

---

[4] Thorpe, *Ancient Laws and Institutes*, vol. II, p. 46, cap. 38.
[5] For details of these festivities, see Section 7.

secular entertainments accompanying Rogation continued to grow more extravagant and boisterous, and the same complaints about raucous entertainments on the Days of Rogation were being levied in the late twelfth century.

Again, early in the period, Bede complained about the amusements of the nuns of Coldingham: 'Nam et domunculae, quae ad orandum uel legendum factae erant, nunc in comesationum, potationum, fabulationum et ceterarum sunt inlecebrarum cubilia conuersae' ('And the cells that were built for praying and for reading have become haunts of feasting, drinking, gossip, and other delights').[6]

The same complaints were still being expressed centuries later. Lanfranc thundered his disapproval of the monks of Canterbury:

> Monachi Cantuarienses, sicut omnes tunc temporis in Anglia, secularibus haud absimiles erant, nisi quod pudicitiam non facile proderent. Canum cursibus auocari; auium predam raptu aliarum uolucrum per inane sequi. Spumantis equi tergum premere, tesseras quatere, potibus indulgere. Delicatiori uictu et accuratiori cultu, frugalitatem nescire, parsimoniam abnuere. Et cetera id genus, ut magis illos consules quam monachos pro frequentia famulantium diceres.

> (The monks of Canterbury, like all monks at that period, were hardly to be distinguished from lay persons, except by their reluctance to betray their chastity. They wasted time hunting with hounds; they pursued avian prey by setting raptors on them in the empty air; they straddled the back of the foaming steed, shook dice, drank deep; too choosy in their diet and too elaborate in their dress, they did not know the meaning of frugality, and refused to be sparing; and so on – you might, from the size of their staff, have thought them consuls rather than monks.)[7]

If entertainment and merriment were abundant even in the halls of monasteries, they must have been still more abundant in the secular world.

The Anglo-Saxon liking for amusement and merriment is also reflected in vocabulary, which has even more terms for 'joy/pleasure/delight' than it has for drinking. In Old English these included *bliss, bliþnes, dream, eadwela, estnes fægennes, (ge)fea, gefeannes, gefeohtsumnes, (ge)glædnes, glædscipe, gliwstæf, hyhtwynn, liss, reotu, gesælignes wynsummung, bleofæstnes, (ge)cwemnes, leof, lust, (ge)lustfullung, myrgen, neod, scyrtung, willa,* and finally *wynn.*[8]

---

[6] Bede, *Bede's Ecclesiastical History*, ed. Colgrave and Mynors, pp. 424–25 (iv. 25).

[7] William of Malmesbury, *Gesta Pontificum Anglorum*, ed. Winterbottom, vol. I, pp. 104–05 (Book i cap. 44.1).

[8] This list is borrowed from Harbus, 'Joy', p. 191, who in turn has extracted the list from the *Dictionary of Old English Web Corpus*. See also Fabiszak, *The Concept of 'Joy'*; Diller, 'Joy and Mirth'; and Gómez and Javier, 'Mixing Pleasure and Beauty'.

The fact that *wynn* (joy) was the name of one of the runes, and that the runes were generally named after very common words and things, may suggest the fundamental position that joy held in the Anglo-Saxon world (or, at least, that it held among nouns beginning with *w*). Two further conjunctions of feelings and delights may support that finding. In the first example, the term *dream* denoted both 'joy' and 'music', and the joy generally described by *dream* is, as Antonina Harbus has put it, 'specifically noisy and exuberant types of joy'.[9] A second instance is the term *gamen*, denoting 'joy/pleasure/mirth', but also 'game'. The two meanings were so closely related that the poem *Maxims I* uses the meaning in a double sense when it depicts two men sitting together dispelling their downheartedness with a board game: 'habban him gomen on borde' ('they shall have joy/a game at the board').[10]

Much joy, then, in Anglo-Saxon England was 'noisy and exuberant', was 'out loud'. Internal, quiet, and beatific joy was reserved for spiritual contexts; but when secular joy and merriment are mentioned, they are communal and apparent. Indeed the communal nature of Anglo-Saxon merriment was one of its most prominent features.[11] Lone figures are sombre ones – hermits like St Guthlac – or miserable ones, such as the gloomy and solitary exiles depicted in *The Wife's Lament* and *The Wanderer*. In one famous instance, those who are alone are literally monsters, as described by *Maxims II*: 'Þyrs sceal on fenne gewunian ana innan lande' ('A monster shall dwell in the fen, alone in the land').[12] Grendel, dwelling almost alone in the forlorn countryside, is stirred to rage by the sounds of communal joy in the hall: it is as if a creature opposed to such joy is literally a monster.

When the Anglo-Saxons were merry, they were in a group, and when they were in a group, they were often merry. Entertainment fostered both merriment and community, and in that sense strengthened society as a whole. It particularly strengthened the bonds of the groups within society, whether those were of the elite, the lowly, the young, the women, or even the religious. And though the meaning of *peorð* may be irrecoverable, the sources of merriment as a whole remain. This Element will explore those sources and seek to bring that merriment to life once more.

---

[9] Harbus, 'Joy', p. 193; see pp. 193–95 on *dream*. See also Dick, '*Æ. dream*'. *Dream* also occasionally denoted less euphonous sounds, meaning something like 'ruckus', but its primary meanings were positive.

[10] Muir, *Exeter Anthology of Old English Poetry*, I.256 (*Maxims I*(C), line 182/44).

[11] On this, see also Bayless, 'Merriment'.

[12] Dobbie, *Anglo-Saxon Minor Poems*, p. 56, lines 43–44.

2 Child's Play

> ' ... ideo uobis licentiam do modo hac uice
> iocandi usque ad signum uespertinum.'
> 'Bene est nobis modo, quod uiuimus.'
> ('I now give you permission this time to play until
> the vespers signal.'
> 'Now it's good for us to be alive!')
> — the *Colloquy* of Ælfric Bata[13]

It is certain that Anglo-Saxon children played and amused themselves, but the play of such a culture leaves little trace in the archaeological record, and almost as little in literature.[14] Many, if not most, games required no specially designed pieces or toys, and the objects used as toys were made of everyday items that would not show up in the archaeological record. The inventiveness of medieval children without manufactured toys is well depicted by several later commentators. Gerald of Wales described his childhood playing outside with his brothers: 'tribus aliis nunc castra nunc oppida nunc palatia puerilibus, ut solet haec aetas, praeludiis in sabulo vel pulvere protrahentibus construentibus, modulo suo, solus hie simili praeludio semper ecclesias eligere et monasteria construere tota intentione satagebat'[15] ('when the other three, preluding the pursuits of manhood in their childish play, were tracing or building, in sand or dust, now towns, now palaces, he himself, in like prophetic play, was ever busy with all his might in designing churches or building monasteries'[16]).

And the author of the fifteenth-century Scots poem *Ratis Raving* described children

> with flouris for to Jap, and plays
> With stikis and with spalys small
> To byge vp chalmer, spens & hall;
> To mak a wicht horse of a wand,
> Of brokin breid a schip saland
> A bunwed tyll a burly spere,
> And of a seg a swerd of were
> a cumly lady of a clout,

---

[13] Ælfric Bata, *Anglo-Saxon Conversations*, pp. 94–95.

[14] Children's toys and games of the later medieval period are better documented; on those, with occasional references to the Anglo-Saxon period, see Orme, *Medieval Children*, pp. 164–97; Lewis, 'Children's Play', and Harper, 'Toys'. An examination of Scandinavian childhood parallel to the Anglo-Saxon period is available in McGuire, 'Whim Rules the Child'.

[15] Gerald of Wales, *De rebus a se gestis* I.i, p. 21.

[16] Gerald of Wales, *Autobiography*, p. 35 (Book I cap. I).

and be rycht besy thar-bout.
To dicht It fetesly with flouris
And luf the pepane paramouris.[17]

(playing and having fun with flowers, with sticks and bits, to build up a chamber,
buttery, and hall; to make a white horse from a stick, a sailing ship of broken bread,
[turn] a ragwort stem into a stout spear, and from a sedge, a sword of war; a comely
lady from cloth, and be very busy about it, to deck it elegantly with flowers, and
cherish the lovely doll.)

None of this activity would have shown up in the archaeology, but it is testimony to the inventiveness of children, and to how their playful industry escapes
most official records.

Perhaps most available of all the easily available things, sticks could easily
be fashioned into toys. In an Old English expansion of the *Consolation of
Philosophy*, Alfred described children using sticks as hobby horses: 'Ða cild
ridað on heora stafum ⁊ manigfealde plegan plegiað þær hi onhyriað ealdum
monnum'[18] ('The children ride on their sticks and play many games where
they imitate adults'). Similarly the *Colloquies* of Ælfric Bata describe games
with sticks, hoops, and whips to roll them, and balls:

'Tu, puer, commoda mihi unum baculum, et ego accommodare uolo tibi duos
baculos statim, si uis.'
'Habeo satis, et si tu uis mecum ludere trocho, ego dabo tibi unum flagellum,
ut in inuicem ambo possimus iocare. Si uis cum pila ludere, commodabo tibi
et pilam meam et baculum meum ad ludendum.'

('You, boy, lend me a stick, and I'll give you back two sticks right away, please.'
'I have plenty. And if you want to play with a hoop together, I'll give you
a flail so we can both play taking turns. If you want to play with a ball, I'll
lend you both my ball and my stick to play with.')[19]

A child with a hoop and stick may be represented on fol. 67v of the Harley
Psalter (of the eleventh century), where a woman is depicted handing a round
object to a boy holding a stick. This has been interpreted as a mother giving
a child a ring, or in other ways, but Sally Crawford has suggested that the
scene may depict a hoop and stick, and illustrate the first phrase of Psalm 131,
which begins directly after the image: 'I do not occupy myself with things too
great and marvellous for me.'[20]

---

[17] Girvan, *Ratis Raving*, pp. 32–33 (lines 1129–39).

[18] Irvine and Godden, *The Old English Boethius*, vol. I, p. 342, with commentary at vol. II, p. 430.
There is also a translation of this passage at vol. II, p. 69, though the translation provided here is
my own.

[19] Ælfric Bata, *Anglo-Saxon Conversations*, pp. 94–95.

[20] Crawford, *Childhood in Anglo-Saxon England*, p. 143.

Other simple play-objects were also used. Playing-balls (*pila ludicra*) are mentioned by Bede;[21] these might be made of leather or of inflated animal bladders, among other substances. Tops were also known. A small top, measuring only 6.9 cm (2.7 inches), was found in an excavation in Winchester; it was pointed at both top and bottom and had a groove for whipping.[22] A whipping top is also mentioned in a curious passage in the Old English version of *Apollonius of Tyre*, in which Apollonius 'swang þone top mid swa micelre swiftnesse' ('whipped the top with so great swiftness').[23]

A more complex toy was a sort of noisemaker made by boring holes in pig metapodia – particular bones of the feet – and whirling the device around to produce a buzzing sound.[24]

Such toys were shaped, but many other playthings were more like sticks: naturally occurring objects turned to the purposes of play. Cherry stones were a popular item in the later Middle Ages, used as playing pieces, counters, primitive marbles, and for many other purposes; it is probable they were similarly popular in the Anglo-Saxon period. The knucklebones of sheep, goats, and other animals have been even more popular in numerous cultures; their shape means that they have six distinct sides, and so they can serve as natural dice, as well as for many other games of catching and dexterity. Neither cherry stones nor knucklebones have much chance, however, of being identified as toys in the archaeological record.

Throughout the Middle Ages most English people carried knives, for eating and for other household purposes, and children apparently received small versions of these essential tools at a young age.[25] Although the knives were necessary for utilitarian purposes, children almost certainly turned them to recreational purposes as well, as it is easy to imagine them whittling their own toys and perhaps practising throwing the knives skilfully, in an early version of the game of

---

[21] Bede, *De temporum ratione liber*, p. 380 (cap. 32.3–10). For more on ball games, which were also played by adults, see Section 7.

[22] Biddle, *Object and Economy*, vol. II, p. 706.

[23] Goolden, *The Old English* Apollonius of Tyre, p. 21. The presence of the top in this scene has caused much confusion. The scene depicts Apollonius and the king in the bathhouse, and in the Latin version Apollonius acts as masseur to the king: 'docta manu ceroma refricuit cum tanta subtilitate' ('with skilled hand rubbed him with the wax with such great finesse'). This passage has been replaced in the Old English version with the description of Apollonius whipping the top. However tempting the interpretation, the description is unlikely to imply something obscene; the options for understanding the wording are explored most fully by Ng, 'Swinging the Top'. Whatever accounts for the passage, it is the first instance of the word *top*, meaning the toy, in English.

[24] Riddler and Trzaska-Nartowsk, 'Chanting upon a Dunghill', p. 131; MacGregor, *Bone, Antler, Ivory and Horn*, pp. 102–03; MacGregor, Mainman, and Rogers, *Craft, Industry, and Everyday Life*, pp. 1980–81.

[25] On these and other goods found in children's graves, see Crawford, 'Children, Grave Goods and Social Status', p. 176.

mumblety-peg. They also turned knives to less innocuous purposes, as Ælfric Bata's *Colloquy* reflects in the dialogue between two boys:

> 'Redde mihi unum cultellum, ut possim cotidie cum eo manducare cibum meum in mea sede cum meis sessoribus in refectorio.'
> 'Tunc, cum ebrius fueris, statim uis transfodere sessorem tuum, puto, cum illo.'

> ('Give me a knife, so every day I can eat my food with it while I sit in my place with my benchmates in the refectory.'
> 'But then when you're drunk, right away you'll want to stab your benchmate with it, I think!')[26]

Child-size swords and spears have also been found in child burials.[27] It is likely that these were placed in the burial for symbolic purposes, rather than as toys, but children must have played with mock weapons as well, probably wooden ones rather than valuable and lethal real ones.

It may even be possible to discern the playthings of infants. The grave of an infant two months or younger, in Great Chesterford, Essex, had a small pot containing a hobnail, and in Farthing Downs, Surrey, a child was buried with a small pot that contained a pebble.[28] These may have served as rattles and, if so, there may have been many more undetected in the archaeological record.

Dolls in later centuries were made of wood, wax, or cloth, and these may well have existed in Anglo-Saxon England. Even less likely to survive would be another substance for making dolls and other items: dough. In later periods rye dough was renowned as a way of making figures, so much so that a commentator of the early modern period reported, 'We have a sayeing, $\left\{ \begin{array}{l} \text{She lookes} \\ \text{He stands} \end{array} \right\}$ like an image of rye-dough.'[29] An eighth-century Continental text also refers to images made of dough or cloth, and although these images were not toys (the text condemns them as idols), it is clearly possible that dolls were made of such substances as well.[30]

Running, acrobatics, and other athletics required no equipment at all. One prominent description of children engaged in such play is found in the *Life of Cuthbert*, where Cuthbert is depicted as preeminent in playground games until scolded:

---

[26] Ælfric Bata, *Anglo-Saxon Conversations*, pp. 114–15.

[27] On this, see, for instance, Crawford, *Childhood*, p. 143.

[28] These are noted by Crawford in 'Children, Grave Goods and Social Status', p. 174, citing Evison, *An Anglo-Saxon Cemetery*, p. 105 and Meaney, *A Gazetteer of Early Anglo-Saxon Burial Sites*, p. 241. Crawford refers to Farthing Downs as 'Farthingdown'.

[29] Aubrey, *Remaines of Gentilisme and Judaisme*, p. 107.

[30] Pertz, *Capitularia regum Francorum*, pp. 19–20 at p. 20, line 14. An English translation can be found in McNeill and Gamer, *Medieval Handbooks of Penance*, pp. 419–20 at p. 420, no. 26.

Dum ergo puer esset annorum octo, omnes coaetaneos in agilitate et petulantia superans, ita ut sepe postquam fessis menbris requiescebant alii, ille adhuc in loco ioci quasi in stadio triumphans aliquem secum ludificantem expectaret. Tunc congregati sunt quadam die multi iuuenes in campi planicie, inter quos ille inuentus est, ioci uarietatem, et scurilitatem agere ceperunt. Alii namque stantes nudi uersis capitibus contra naturam deorsum ad terram, et expansis cruribus erecti pedes ad coelos sursum prominebant. Alii sic, alii uero sic fecerunt.

(When he was a boy of eight years, he surpassed all of his age in agility and high spirits, so that often, after the others had gone to rest their weary limbs, he, standing triumphantly in the playground as though he were in the arena, would still wait for someone to play with him. At that time many youths were gathered together one day on a piece of level ground and he too was found among them. They began thereupon to indulge in a variety of games and tricks; some of them stood naked, with their heads turned down unnaturally towards the ground, their legs stretched out and their feet lifted up and pointed skywards; and some did one thing and some another.)[31]

The practice of children playing naked may have been commonplace and it stretched on for centuries beyond the Anglo-Saxon period; it is depicted, for instance, in an illustration accompanying the verb form *ludo* ('I play') in Uppsala, University Library C 678, fol. 126v, dating from 1475–1500, where a group of children are playing with a ball and ninepins, a whipping top, a whirligig, a toy bird, and turning themselves upside down, all of the children naked. Going naked may have been especially useful for children who were not yet toilet trained, or it may have been merely expedient not to expose precious clothing (of which each child had probably only a single set) to rough-and-tumble play at a rough-and-tumble time of life.

Older youths also enjoyed athletics and races. The *Vita* of Wulfstan, Bishop of Worcester (*c.* 1008–1095), surviving in a later version by William of Malmesbury, described sports on the village green:

Conuenerat in campum frequens cetus adolescentum, cuinam letius ludo uacans non diffinio. Cursitabatur ut fieri solet in talibus uirentis graminis aequore, plausui et fauori adhortantium respondebat stridulus aer.

(A large throng of young people had gathered in a field. I'm not sure what their favored leisure-time sport was – no doubt the usual kind of races on the level greensward. The air resounded loud with applause and acclamation for the contestants.)[32]

The youths in this instance were at least adolescents, as the scene of wholesome athletics is interrupted by the unlikely appearance of a seductive young woman who

---

[31] Colgrave, *The Anonymous Life of St Cuthbert*, book I cap. III, in *Two Lives of St Cuthbert*, pp. 64–65.
[32] *Vita Wulfstani*, i.I.6–7 in *William of Malmesbury: Saints' Lives*, p. 18; translation by Swanton, *Three Lives*, p. 94.

tries to tempt the young Wulfstan into lust. Although he resists the temptation, presumably this means that he was old enough to have something to resist.

Verbal games were also popular among the young, as among their elders. In praising the young St Guthlac, the author of the *Life* describes the common utterances of the people:

> Non puerorum lascivias, non garrula matronarum deliramenta, non vanas vulgi fabulas, non ruricolarum bardigiosos vagitus, non falsidicas parasitorum fribulas, non variorum volucrum diversos crocitus, ut adsolet illa aetas, imitabatur.

> (He did not imitate the impudence of the children nor the nonsensical chatter of the matrons, nor the empty tales of the common people, nor the foolish shouts of the rustics, nor the lying trifles of flatterers, nor the different cries of the various kinds of birds as children of that age are wont to do.)[33]

Many verbal games must have been lost to history, but one survives in the *Colloquy* of Ælfric Bata: that of hurling insults at each other. This too may have been in imitation of an adult form of verbal play, the flyting, but the urge to hurl insults at another party does not require the existence of a formal genre. The dialogue of insults as reflected by Ælfric Bata rings the changes on the standards of the insult repertoire:

> Tu sochors! Tu scibalum hedi! Tu scibalum ouis! Tu scibalum equi! Tu fimus bouis! Tu stercus porci! Tu hominis stercus! Tu canis scibalum! Tu uulpis scibalum! Tu muricipis stercus! Tu galline stercus! ... Habe scibalum in barba tua et in ore tuo stercus et scibalum tria et duo, octo et unum, et ego nullum, habeto semper.

> (You idiot! You goat shit! Sheep shit! Horse shit! You cow dung! You pig turd! You human turd! You dog shit! Fox shit! Cat turd! Chicken shit! ... May you always have shit in your beard, and shit and turds in your mouth, three and two times and eight and one, and I none at all ever!)[34]

Fun evidently could be imported even into the learning of Latin.

Certain holidays became a special occasion for children's games. In later centuries, playing with whipping tops became almost a ritual for Easter, associated with the flagellation of Christ during the Passion. It is not clear whether this tradition had started in the Anglo-Saxon period. The festivities on St John's Eve, also known as midsummer eve, however, included children's games. The earliest attestation comes from an eleventh-century life of St Edith from Wilton Abbey, describing a teenage boy distracted by the traditional games of St John's Eve: 'nocturnis puerorum ludis, qui in eadem festiuitate iuxta ritum antiquorum

---

[33] Felix, *Felix's Life of St Guthlac*, pp. 78–79.
[34] Ælfric Bata, *Anglo-Saxon Conversations*, pp. 138–39.

sollemniter celebrantur, quadam animi leuitate uacare cepit'[35] ('he started to abandon [the vigil], engaging with a certain lightness of mind in the nighttime games of the boys, which are celebrated with due ceremony at that festival according to ancient practice').

A witness from the late thirteenth century recalled the tradition of games on St John's Eve in Barnwell, near Cambridge, with the implication that their practice in Anglo-Saxon times gave the village its name, *bearn wyll*, 'the well of the children':

> Pueri et adolescentes, ... illic convenientes, more Anglorum luctamina et alia ludicra exercebant puerilia, et cantilenis et musicis instrumentis sibi invicem applaudebant, unde propter turbam puerorum et puellarum illic concurrentium, mos inolevit ut in eodem die illic conveniret negotiandi gratia turba vendentium et ementium.

> (according to the custom of the English ... boys and youths ... assembled there, and practised wrestling and other boyish games, and mutually applauded one another with songs and musical instruments; whence, on account of the multitude of boys and girls who gathered there, it grew a custom for a crowd of sellers and other buyers to assemble there on the same day for the purpose of commerce.)[36]

These great childhood festivities may stand in for the greater bulk of childhood play and recreation in this early period, the great energy and enjoyment of which so little trace survives. Children made their playthings out of the basic and informal materials to hand, and of what must have been innumerable games and sports, only the briefest mention makes it into the records. These show, however, that play and enjoyment were pursued across the entire lifespan, from the earliest baby's rattles to the more elaborate entertainments for which childhood was just a rehearsal.

3 Drinking and Feasting

> Sum sceal on heape   hæleþum cweman,
> blissian æt beore   bencsittendum;
> þær biþ drincendra   dream se micla.

> (One shall serve in the company of heroes,
> rejoicing at beer with the bench-sitters;
> there is a great joy among the drinkers there!)
> — *The Fortunes of Men* 77–84

---

[35] Wilmart, 'La légende de Ste Édithe', p. 301.

[36] The passage was noted by Crawford in *Childhood in Anglo-Saxon England*, pp. 140 and 184, n. 6, citing Wright, *A History of Domestic Manners*, p. 67. Wright supplies this translation and gives the original passage in Latin from British Library, Harley 3601, fol. 12v. It is not clear if or where this text from Harley 3601 is otherwise published.

Cornu bibere uolo. Cornu habere debeo,
cornu tenere. Cornu uocor. Cornu est nomen
meum. Cum cornu uiuere, cornu quoque
iacere uolo et dormine, nauigare, equitare
et ambulare et laborare atque ludere.
Omnes propinqui mei et amici cornua
habuerunt et ebiberunt, et mori uolo cum
cornu … Cornu habeo modo. Cornu bibo.
Omne bonum habeto, et cornu bibamus leti
omnes.

(I want to drink from the horn. I ought to have
the horn, to hold the horn. I'm called horn!
Horn is my name! I want to live with the horn,
to lie with the horn and sleep, to sail, ride, walk,
work and play with the horn. All my kith and
kin had horns and drank. And I want to die with
the horn! … Now I have the horn. I'm drinking
from the horn. Have every good thing, and let's
all be happy and drink from the horn!)
          — the *Colloquy* of Ælfric Bata[37]

Many cultures have held feasting and drinking in high esteem, but the Anglo-Saxons were especially famed for their love of such things. This reputation may well have been warranted: the English were enthusiastic drinkers, and the arrangements for feasting and its paraphernalia occupied significant time and resources. Drinking was an indispensable part of feasting, and the arrangements might include a formal dinner, a demonstration of power and wealth, conducted in centres of ecclesiastical power as well as in the great secular households; and it might be an event of music, poetry, boasting, and ribaldry; or it might be as informal and private as the women's drinking parties that scandalised Ælfric: a small assertion of agency, rebellion, and enjoyment. Drinking implied companionship, so much so that a term for a companion was *gebeor*, 'fellow drinker'. In turn, drinking was at the heart of feasting, so that a common word for a feast was *gebeorscipe* or *beorscipe*, a 'beer-companionship'.[38] A *gebeorscipe* became almost a byword for something desirable; in his *Life* of St Cecilia, for instance, Ælfric wrote that the martyrs were so fearless that they 'swa bliþelice eodon to heora agenum slege swylce to gebeorscipe' ('went to their own slaughter as joyfully as to a *gebeorscipe*').[39] The fact that the Last Supper was a communal meal, and that the joys of heaven were often

[37] Ælfric Bata, *Anglo-Saxon Conversations*, pp. 102–03.

[38] A poetic term, less commonly attested, is *beorþegu*, 'beer-drinking', which appears three times in *Beowulf*.

[39] Ælfric, *Ælfric's Lives of Saints*, vol. 2, p. 368, lines 228–29.

portrayed as a banquet with God, meant that feasting had divine sanction as well as secular appeal.

Although in real life many locales provided an opportunity for carousing, in literature the *locus classicus* of joyful community was the hall, with communal drinking at the heart of it. Indeed, the word *hall* often appeared in poetic compounds that highlighted its function as a drinking place, including *meoduheall* (mead hall), *meduseld* (mead hall), *medoærn* (mead hall), *beorsele* (beer hall), *winærn* (wine hall), *winsalo* (wine hall), and *winsele* (wine hall). The hall joys were clearly alcoholic. Beowulf characterised the joy of Heorot as 'mead joy':

> Weorod wæs on wynne;   ne seah ic widan feorh
> under heofones hwealf   healsittendra
> medudream maran. (2014–2016)

> (The warband was joyful; never have I seen in my life under heaven's vault greater mead joy among those who sit in the hall.)

The passage from *The Fortunes of Men*, quoted as the epigraph at the start of this section, reiterates the association, speaking of 'blissian æt beore bencsittendum' ('rejoicing at beer with the bench-sitters'). And in the beginning of *Beowulf*, Scyld's victories are characterised as the destruction of the mead-benches:

> Oft Scyld Scefing   sceaþena þreatum,
> monegum mægþum   meodosetla ofteah (4–5).

> (Often Scyld Scefing deprived bands of enemies, many nations, of their mead-benches.)

The hall, with the lord presiding, formed the location of the feast as a ceremonial display of abundance and wealth, of power and generosity.[40] Secular halls were a natural site for such feasts, but many monastic halls had similar revels, for their own fellowship and particularly when hosting secular lords. Indeed, the *Regularis concordia*, which set out the rules for monastic life, directed that the abbot of a monastery should offer hospitality to guests 'deuotissime', which many abbots did with enthusiasm.[41]

Feasting demanded both leisure and resources, and the person who had the greatest supply of both was the king. Indeed, it has been argued that the *feorm*, the contribution of food and supplies due to the king and nobles, did not consist of food-rents for everyday consumption as has been assumed, but provided the supplies for feasts, and accordingly the term *feorm* denoted a feast as well as

---

[40] On images of the hall as the centre of feasting and drinking, see Magennis, *Images of Community*, pp. 35–103; Brown, 'The Feast Hall in Anglo-Saxon Society', Pollington, 'The Mead-Hall Community', and Gautier, *Le festin dans l'Angleterre anglo-saxonne*.

[41] Symons, *Regularis Concordia*, p. 62.

a supply of food for it.[42] The size these feasts might attain is suggested by a list of supplies making up a *feorm* in the laws of King Ine of Wessex, probably dating from the late seventh or early eighth century. The supply list included 10 vessels of honey, 300 loaves of bread (probably each feeding one person), substantial amounts of butter, 2 kinds of ale, 10 cheeses, 2 cattle or 10 wethers, 10 geese, 20 hens, 5 salmon, and 100 eels.[43] In later centuries the menu expanded. The late Anglo-Saxon feasters at the hall in Portchester ate twenty kinds of wildfowl, and the diners at Waltham Holy Cross were to be supplied with blackbirds, plovers, partridges, and pheasants every week between Michaelmas and Lent.[44] Fish became more available as the commercial fishing industry developed, and the elite classes were 'eating more elegant dishes in a more elegant manner', and their feasts included 'sauces, spicing, white bread, a choice of dishes at every meal, cooks, even serving boys'.[45]

Although all these provisions certainly would have supplied nutrition and energy, the main point of such lavish feasting would have been enjoyment and display. As the authors of one study write, 'it is unlikely that kings attended them because they had a pressing economic need for large quantities of food. It is more probable that these feasts were important in political and symbolic terms; they were special occasions on which a king's legitimacy was publicly recognized and his authority accepted'.[46] But it is also important to keep in mind that the king demonstrated his legitimacy and authority by fostering pleasure and merriment.

Archaeology provides further evidence for the importance of music, feasting, and what must have been communal merriment.[47] The grave goods with which high-status burials of the early period were provided often included the equipment for a feast. The early seventh-century ship burial in Sutton Hoo Mound 1 contained forty-two feasting vessels, including a large silver dish, ten silver bowls, silver spoons, drinking vessels, three cauldrons, three bronze hanging bowls, a lyre, and playing pieces for a board game.[48] This assemblage of peacetime artefacts contrasts with the martial equipment also found in the grave: sword, shield, helmet, and so forth. The presence of both these types of objects suggests that the two spheres of life they represent were given equally high value. The feasting equipment was ornate; the silver objects were made in the Eastern Mediterranean, and possibly

---

[42] Lambert and Leggett, 'Food and Power'; see p. 138 for references to archaeological evidence of feasting pits, for roasting whole animals, from the fifth to the seventh centuries.

[43] The original, in chapter 70.1 of the laws of Ine, is cited in Jurasinski and Oliver, *The Laws of Alfred*, pp. 430–31, clause 72. On the contents, see Lambert and Leggett, 'Food and Power', pp. 6–12; on the date, see Lambert and Leggett, 'Food and Power', p. 6, n. 19.

[44] Fleming, 'The New Wealth', p. 5.   [45] Fleming, 'The New Wealth', p. 7.

[46] Lambert and Legett, 'Food and Power', p. 5.

[47] On feasting equipment in Anglo-Saxon burials, see Lee, *Feasting the Dead*, pp. 72–86.

[48] Bruce-Mitford, *The Sutton Hoo Ship Burial*; Evans, *The Sutton Hoo Ship Burial*.

reached England as gifts, all facts which point to a recognition of feasting as a central feature of life, and perhaps especially suitable to princely life. The late sixth-century princely grave at Taplow displays many of the same features; the grave goods included cups, glasses, drinking horns with silver-gilt mounts, enormous cooking vessels, a lyre, and, once again, playing pieces for a board game.[49] The seventh-century princely burial at Prittlewell yielded similar treasures, with twenty-two vessels for feasting, including thirteen drinking vessels of horn, glass, and wood; a large bowl and an ewer, both of Byzantine make; a 'Celtic' hanging bowl; a large tub; and a cauldron.[50]

Although Anglo-Saxons ceased to be buried with grave goods in the seventh century, the contents of wills suggest that feasting equipment continued to be among the most costly and treasured items of property. Ælfgifu, who made her will sometime between 966 and 975, bequeathed a variety of treasures, including gold coins, bracelets, a necklace, horses, spears, shields, and estates. Sop cups – cups in which bread could be dipped into wine or water – formed part of her valuables, and she left one to the king, another to the queen, and a third sop cup and an ornamented drinking horn to others.[51] One wonders whether these commemorated feasts in which Ælfgifu celebrated with the royal couple, or whether they had purely symbolic value. The will of Ælfheah, written between 968 and 971, includes a dish and a sop cup worth three pounds each, as well as coins, horses, spears, shields, and a dagger with a valuable hilt.[52] In both these instances, as in a number of others, the equipment for feasting and merriment had equal status with martial equipment, and often formed a canvas for the expression of wealth and connections to power.

Many such feasts might have been enjoyed when the kings were on circuit, circulating through the countryside. Eddius Stephanus' *Life of Wilfrid* depicts the seventh-century king Ecgfrith and his queen feasting and merry-making on circuit: 'rex cum regina sua per civitates et castellas vicosque cotidie gaudentes et epulantes in pompa saeculari circumeuntes'[53] ('the king together with the queen going on circuit through the cities and fortresses and villages, with worldly pomp and rejoicing and feasting every day'). The description is meant to illustrate the impiety of the royal couple, as they have spurned Wilfrid, but their actions were probably typical for a couple of their status.

Feasting might also take place on many other occasions, from the grand, such as the coronation of Edward the Confessor in 1042, celebrated with feasting and

---

[49] Stevens, 'On the Remains Found in an Anglo-Saxon Tumulus at Taplow'.
[50] Webster, 'The Prittlewell (Essex) Burial'.
[51] Whitelock, *Anglo-Saxon Wills*, pp. 20–21 (no. VIII).
[52] Whitelock, *Anglo-Saxon Wills*, pp. 22–24 (no. IX).
[53] Eddius Stephanus, *The Life of Bishop Wilfrid*, p. 78 (cap. XXXIX).

drinking,[54] to the more local, as when the church at Ripon was completed and the local kings marked the occasion with three days of feasting;[55] or the feast in an ordinary house which a travelling Briton happened to attend, ultimately proving the sanctity of the relics of Oswald when the house caught fire and the feast was disrupted;[56] or even the very informal, as the cleric Ælfsige used to enjoy *epulis*, 'feast dishes', under his favourite tree.[57] Although the conventional modern vision of the feast portrays it as an occasion where the elite consume the tribute of the lowly in a display of power in the hall, the lowly certainly had their own feasts, some indeed supplied by the elite. The eleventh-century *Rectitudines* outlined some of these occasions, specifying the kinds of feasts that might be owed to farmworkers, including 'bendfeorm for ripe, gytfeorm for yrðe, mæðmed, hreacmete, æt wudulade wæntreow, æt cornlade hreaccopp'[58] ('a binding-feast for harvest, a drinking-feast at ploughing, a mowing-reward, a rick-meal, at wood-carrying a log, at corn-carrying a rick-cup'). These might have taken place in the barns, in the farmyard, or even in the fields themselves.

Commercial drinking establishments might also provide opportunities for carousing. It is unclear whether these were year-round establishments or, as often appeared in later medieval England, houses that brewed ale on an occasional basis and opened their doors to paying drinkers when they were in supply. Such establishments turn up in prohibitions, as they were clearly popular. The laws of Æthelred specified the penalties to be paid for violating the peace 'on ealahuse' ('in an alehouse'), suggesting unsurprisingly that alehouses might be scenes of rowdiness.[59] Winehouses also appear in the work of Ælfric, who decreed: 'Ne mot nan preost beon mangere oþþe gerefa. Ne drincan æt wynhuse, ne druncen-georn beon'[60] ('No priest is allowed to be a merchant or a reeve, or to drink at a winehouse, or to be drunk'). And *The Seasons for Fasting* complains about the priest who celebrates mass and then goes straight to the tapster (*æfter tæppere*) and orders wine and oysters, drinking merrily and assuring others that it is not sinful to do so.[61]

Although such occasions do not quite qualify as 'entertainment', it was also the custom to drink at wakes.[62] Ælfric was particularly exercised about the impropriety of this, warning against eating and drinking at wakes in his letter to

[54] Barlow, *Edward the Confessor*, p. 64.
[55] Eddius Stephanus, *The Life of Bishop Wilfrid*, p. 35 (cap. XVII).
[56] Bede, *Bede's Ecclesiastical History*, ed. Colgrave and Mynors, pp. 244–45 (iii.x).
[57] William of Malmesbury, *Saints' Lives*, ed. Winterbottom and Thomson, pp. 94–97.
[58] *Rectitudines singularum personarum* 21.4, in Liebermann, *Die Gesetze der Angelsachsen*, vol. I, pp. 452–53.
[59] Liebermann, *Die Gesetze der Angelsachsen*, vol. I, p. 228 (III Æthelred 1,2).
[60] Ælfric, *Die Hirtenbriefe Aelfrics*, p. 134 (Brief II, nos. 185–86).
[61] *The Seasons for Fasting*, 208–20, 224–30. in Dobbie, *The Anglo-Saxon Minor Poems*, p. 104. On further evidence for Anglo-Saxon alehouses, see Hagen, *A Second Handbook*, pp. 245–46.
[62] On drinking and feasting connected with funerary rites, see Lee, *Feasting the Dead*.

Wulfsige,[63] while in the *Life of St Swithun* he lamented that 'Sume menn eac drincað æt deadra manna lice ofer ealle þa niht swiðe unrihtlice and gremiað God mid heora gegafspræcum, þonne nan gebeorscipe ne gebyrað æt lice, ac halige gebedu þær gebyriað swiþor'[64] ('some men most wrongfully drink all through the night at dead men's corpses and anger God with their buffoonery, whereas no beer-drinking is proper at the corpse, but rather holy prayers are more appropriate there'). Similarly the *Canons of Edgar* warned: 'And riht is þæt man æt cyricwæccan swyðe dreoh sy, and georne gebidde, and ænig gedrync ne ænig unnytt ðær ne dreoge'[65] ('And it is right that one should be very sober at church vigils, and pray devoutly, and refrain from drinking or indulging in any inanities there'). A more formal funerary feast might also be celebrated. The late Anglo-Saxon will of a man named Wægen, from Bury St Edmunds, specified the supplies for his initial funerary feast: bread, a pig, a bullock, three bucks, cheese, fish, and milk.[66] Commemorative feasts might also be held in later years, such as that for Badanoth Beotting, who donated land to the community at Christ Church, Canterbury in the eighth century to supply the resources for a feast to be held on the anniversaries of his death.[67]

Although many feasts were clearly ostentatious affairs, feasting and drinking might also be clandestine. Alcuin warned the monks of Wearmouth-Jarrow against such pleasure-seeking: 'Absconditas commessationes et furtivas ebrietates quasi foveam inferni vitate'[68] ('Shun secret feasting and furtive drunkenness like the pit of hell'). In Ælfric's letter to Brother Eadweard, it is not the lowly monks but the countrywomen who are sneaking off to carouse in secret: 'ic hit gehyrde oft secgan ... þæt þas uplendiscan wif wyllað oft drincan and furþon etan fullice on gangsetlum æt heora gebeorscipum'[69] ('I have heard it often said, that countrywomen will often drink and even eat foully on the toilet seats at their feasts'). One wonders why the women would choose such a disagreeable place for their celebrations; the reason may well be that such a place was blessedly off-limits to interfering authorities such as Ælfric.

More formal feasts included a certain degree of ritual. Manuscript images and other sources, such as Tatwine's riddle 29, suggest that a white cloth covered the table at formal meals. The drink served might be high-status wine or the lower-status but more common *beor* and *ealu*. Ale came in several varieties: '"Welsh,"

---

[63] Ælfric, *Die Hirtenbriefe Aelfrics*, p. 25 (Brief I, 113).
[64] Lapidge, *The Cult of St Swithun*, pp. 602–03.
[65] Wulfstan, *Wulfstan's Canons of Edgar*, p. 9, no. 28.
[66] Robertson, *Anglo-Saxon Charters*, p. 252; Lee, *Feasting the Dead*, p. 112.
[67] Robertson, *Anglo-Saxon Charters*, p. 10 (no. VI); Lee, *Feasting the Dead*, pp. 111–12.
[68] Dümmler, *Epistolae Karolini Aevi* II, p. 55 (no. 19).
[69] Clayton, 'An Edition of Ælfric's *Letter to Brother Edward*', p. 282.

"pure or clear," "new," "old," "twice-brewed," "sweet," and "sour"'.[70] Some idea of the foods available may be garnered from the lists of *feorm* and other supplies, and included venison, beef, pork, mutton, geese, chicken, wild birds such as cranes and partridges, fish, eels, milk, butter, cheese, honey, and bread. The less common of these probably served as delicacies. Bishop Wulfstan, for instance, shunned all meat after being tempted by the delectable aroma of roast goose, 'Si qua tamen esset caro delectabilis, opinari se quod alaudae maiorem uescentibus darent uoluptatem' ('But [he said] if any flesh could give pleasure, larks were the best fare').[71]

The amount of meat in such feasts was no doubt much greater than that in the average person's diet, but few of the foodstuffs of the feast were exotic, unlike, for instance, the situation on the Continent, where Charlemagne was accustomed to feasting on peacock.[72] However plain or extravagant the ingredients, the preparation may have been much more elaborate for feasts; but more precise evidence for cooking and spicing – for recipes – does not survive from this period.[73]

Images of the period show that in formal feasts, the elite sat on one side of the table, served from the opposite side, and that the table was laid with a white cloth. Once the diners were in place, the drinking began when the wife of the man with the highest status served the drink. As Donald Bullough has observed:

> The queen's ritual offering of drink – with which the drinking-vessels in graves may (or may not) be connected – is not merely a gesture of hospitality, establishing her own status; it also establishes precedence in the hall and emphasises that the real and fictive kin who form the warrior-band are none the less their lord's subordinates, with a hierarchy among themselves based on birth, age and achievement.[74]

Maxims I described the ceremony, portraying the wife of an *eorl* at her duties, where she approaches the lord first among the company with a full cup (87–91). Hrothgar's wife Wealtheow performs such a ceremony in *Beowulf* (612–28 and 2016–21).[75]

This ritual reveals another feature of such feasts: the fact that the texts specify the order in which she brings the vessel to the drinkers show that the participants must be drinking from the same cup. The problem of a drinker partaking too heartily from the shared cup, and leaving less for his fellow drinkers, was tackled by Dunstan. William of Malmesbury reported:

---

[70] Quoted from Doyle, 'Beer and Ale', p. 44. See also Fell, 'Old English *Beor*'.
[71] William of Malmesbury, *Gesta Pontificum Anglorum*, ed. and trans. Winterbottom, vol. I, pp. 424–25 (iv.139.2).
[72] Chandler, 'Charlemagne's Table'. I am grateful to Eileen Morgan for this reference.
[73] On this, see Gautier, 'Cooking and Cuisine'.
[74] Bullough, *Friends, Neighbours and Fellow-drinkers*, p. 16.
[75] The tradition is surveyed, with rather romantic claims about cultic and mystical origins, by Enright in *Lady with a Mead Cup*.

quia compatriotae in tabernis conuenientes iamque temulenti pro modo bibendi contenderent, ipse clauos argenteos uel aureos iusserit uasis affigi, ut, dum metam suam quisque cognosceret, non plus subseruiente uerecundia uel ipse appeteret uel alium appetere cogeret.

(seeing how his compatriots gathered in taverns and, when already flown with wine, fought over the amount that each should drink, he ordered that pins of silver or gold should be fixed in the drinking-vessels, so that each man could recognize his own proper limit, and not forget his good manners and either demand more for himself or compel another man to do so).[76]

The practice must have continued for some time; a church council of 1102 decreed 'Vt presbiteri non eant ad potationes nec ad pinnas bibant'[77] ('That priests should not go to carousals, or drink to the pins').

There was also a conventional ritual of saluting fellow drinkers. As described by numerous witnesses, the first drinker exclaimed 'Wæs hæl!' ("Be healthy!"), to which the response was 'Drinc hæl!' ('Drink healthy!').[78] In later centuries, the *wæs hæl* of the formula evolved into the term 'wassail'. This practice suggests that the drinkers were each drinking from their own cups, so perhaps this call-and-response was used after the initial circulation of the communal drinking vessel. Whenever it occurred, it must have encouraged the drinkers to partake of ever more draughts.

The rest of the feast provided additional opportunities for enjoyment and the display of status and power. One can assume that the seating reflected status; in cognate cultures, violence often broke out from disputes over the seating.[79] The giving out of portions of food also reflected social hierarchy. Elite sites where feasting must have taken place feature disproportionate finds of hunted red and roe deer, suggesting a ritual presentation and an understanding that the head of the animal is most appropriate for the 'head' of the group.[80] It has been argued that the division of venison at a feast resembled the ritual distribution of war spoils, making such occasions a display of masculine power. In this regard the name of Hrothgar's hall in *Beowulf*, 'Heorot' (hart, or male red deer), serves to emphasise masculine power.[81] The seax, or short sword, may be related to these. Seaxes often have

---

[76] William of Malmesbury, *Gesta Regum Anglorum*, vol. I, pp. 240–41 (Book II, cap. 149.2).

[77] William of Malmesbury, *Gesta Pontificum Anglorum*, ed. Winterbottom and Thomson, vol. I, pp. 190–93 (Book I cap. 64.5).

[78] Geoffrey of Monmouth provided the tradition with a backstory relating it to Rowena, the supposed daughter of Hengist: *The Historia regum Britannie*, vol. 1, §99, p. 67. Later works such as Lagamon's *Brut* and Robert of Gloucester's *Chronicle* repeated the legend. The tradition (without any reference to Hengist or Rowena) is also attested by Gerald of Wales (*Speculum Ecclesiae* Book III, cap. xiv in *Giraldi Cambrensis Opera*, vol. 4, pp. 209, 213–14) and the fourteenth-century *Eulogium Historiarum*, ed. Haydon, vol. III, p. 110 (a. 1216).

[79] Bullough, *Friends, Neighbours and Fellow-drinkers*, pp. 12, 15.

[80] On all of this, see Sykes, 'Deer, Land, Knives and Halls', pp. 180–81.

[81] Marvin, *Hunting Law and Ritual*, pp. 32–34; Sykes, 'Deer', p. 177.

ornately decorated blades, suggesting that they were intended for ceremonial use, such as the carving of meat, rather than for more utilitarian use in war.[82] This would possibly indicate a ritual aspect to the ceremony, in view of carvings such as the futhork inscribed on the Thames scramasax, which has been thought to have been intended to lend the piece a talismanic or protective function.

The feast was often accompanied by entertainment: music, singing, storytelling, riddle-guessing, innuendo, and professional and amateur foolery. Many of these were also present at less formal drinking parties. In the tenth century, King Edgar complained about clerics who 'diffluant in comessationibus et ebrietatibus, in cubilibus et impudicitiis; ut jam domus clericorum putentur prostibula meretricum, conciliabulum histrionum. Ibi aleae, ibi saltus et cantus, ibi usque ad medium noctis spatium protractae in clamore et horrore vigiliae'[83] ('expend themselves in feasting and drinking sessions, in beds and acts of shamelessness; so that now the houses of the clerics are considered brothels of prostitutes, gathering-places for performers. There gaming takes place, there dancing and singing, there people are awake until the middle of the night with loud noise and uncouth behaviour').

These sound like less formal occasions than the ceremonial feasts of the secular elite, although they imitated those in the degree of licence. The complaint also forms a rare witness to the fact that feasting might include dancing as part of the festivities.

However beloved the opportunity for carousing, excessive drinking came under predictable censure.[84] The *Canons of Edgar* asserted 'riht is þæt preostas beorgan wið oferdruncen and hit georne belean oðrum mannum' ('it is right that priests guard against drunkenness and eagerly censure it in other men').[85] *The Fortunes of Men* painted a foreboding portrait of the drunkard:

> Sum sceal on beore þurh byreles hond
> meodugal mæcga; þonne he gemet ne con
> gemearcian his muþe mode sine,
> ac sceal ful earmlice ealdre linnan,
> dreogan dryhtenbealo dreamum biscyred,
> ond hine to sylfcwale secgas nemnað,
> mænað mid muþe meodugales gedrinc. (ll. 51–57)

('One shall be in his beer through the hand of the cup-bearer, a mead-crazed warrior; then he knows no measure in restraining his tongue in his own mind, and shall yield up his life very wretchedly, suffer great ills, cut off from joys, and men call him a self-killer; they mourn with their mouths the drinking of the mead-crazed.')

---

[82] Gale, 'The Seax', p. 74; Sykes, 'Deer', p. 182.

[83] Birch, *Cartularium Saxonicum*, vol. III, p. 573.

[84] On ecclesiastical complaints about excessive drinking and feasting, see Magennis, *Anglo-Saxon Appetites*, pp. 85–128.

[85] Wulfstan, *Wulfstan's Canons of Edgar*, pp. 14–15, no. 58.

Beowulf praises the hero because he never killed any of his fellow drinkers at a drunken feast, a claim which could apparently not be made of all men:

> Swa bealdode   bearn Ecgðeowes,
> guma guðum cuð,   godum dædum,
> dreah æfter dome,   nealles druncne slog
> heorðgeneatas . . . (2177–80)

> ('Thus the son of Ecgtheow was bold,
> a man known for his worthy deeds in battle,
> he achieved glory, never slew his drunken
> hearth companions.')

The potential for drunken violence applied even to schoolboys, as reflected in the *Colloquy* of Ælfric Bata, where one boy surmises that as soon as the other is drunk, he will start using his knife to stab his benchmate.[86]

Despite these cautionary passages, it was generally acknowledged that a certain amount of drinking was customary, indeed inevitable, and sometimes might even be divinely sanctioned.[87] The wine in the eucharist represented the body of Christ, after all, and the miracle of the wedding at Cana showed that the provision of wine had divine approval. While warning against excessive drinking, Aldhelm acknowledged that some drinking was usual, cautioning his correspondent Æthilwald against indulgence 'siue in cotidianis potationibus et conuiuiis usu frequentiore ac prolixiore inhoneste superfluis' ('whether in the excessive practice of daily drinking bouts and parties, taken to disgraceful extremes)'[88] or in other inadvisable activities; but the implication is that partaking in moderate *potationibus et conuiuiis*, not excessive or taken to disgraceful extremes, was usual. Indeed, Godfrey of Jumièges, abbot of Malmesbury in the late eleventh century, even came under fire for excessive sobriety: 'Frugalitate sobrius, et, ut dicebatur, nimius, ut qui, sepe quantum ad se uno contentus ferculo, non temere nisi semel inter prandium et caenam biberet' ('He was sober and frugal, and even (it was said) took this too far, for he often contented himself with a single course, and would not lightly take more than one drink between lunch and dinner').[89]

Miracles depicted a divine abundance of wine, as was the case when King Eadred visited the monastery of Æthelwold, recounted in the *Life of St Æthelwold*:

---

[86] Ælfric, *Anglo-Saxon Conversations*, pp. 114–15.

[87] On this, see Magennis, 'The *Beowulf* Poet and his "druncne dryhtguman"' and Fahey, 'The Wonders of Ebrietas'.

[88] Quoted by William of Malmesbury, *Gesta Pontificum*, ed. Winterbottom, vol. I, pp. 512–13 (Book V, cap. 193.2).

[89] William of Malmesbury, *Gesta Pontificum*, ed. Winterbottom, vol. I, pp. 646–47 (Book V, cap. 271.4).

QVOD REX EADREDVS AD MONASTERIVM VENERIT ET
HOSPITIBVS TOTA DIE BIBENTIBVS LIQVOR EXHAVRIVI
NEQVIVERIT .... rogauitque eum abbas in hospicio cum suis prandere.
Annuit rex ilico; et contigit adesse sibi non paucos optimatum suorum
uenientes ex gente Northanhimbrorum, qui omnes cum rege adierunt con-
uiuium. Laetatusque est rex, et iussit abunde propinare hospitibus
ydromellum .... . Quid multa? Hauserunt ministri liquorem tota die ad
omnem sufficientiam conuiuantibus; sed nequiuit ipse liquori exhauriri de
uase, nisi ad mensuram palmi, inebriatis suatim Northanimbris et uesperi cum
laetitia recedentibus.

(THAT KING EADRED CAME TO THE MONASTERY, AND THOUGH
THE GUESTS DRANK ALL DAY THE DRINK COULD NOT BE
EXHAUSTED .... . the abbot invited him to dine with his people in the
hospice. The king was quick to accept. Now it chanced that he had with him
not a few of his Northumbrian thegns, and they all accompanied him to the
party. The king was delighted, and ordered the guests to be served with lavish
draughts of mead .... . Well, the servants drew off drink all day to the hearts'
content of the diners, but the level in the container could not be reduced below
a palm's measure. The Northumbrians became drunk, as they tend to, and
very cheerful they were when they left at evening.)[90]

A similar story is told by Goscelin in his *Vita S. Wulfhildae*.[91] The motif also
appears in the *Vita S. Dunstani*, where the king and his retinue, dining at the
house of a widow, are unable to exhaust the store of drink despite copious
consumption, and become chastened at burdening their hostess, a miracle which
is attributed to the Virgin Mary.[92] In all these instances, the abundance of wine is
seen as an instance of divine intervention and, by implication, the copious
drinking of wine has divine approval.

The letters of disapproval from church authorities show that the carousing of
clerics was no less enthusiastic than that of laymen. In a letter to Ecgberht,
bishop of York, in 734, Bede expressed concern that certain bishops surrounded
themselves with men 'qui risui, iocis, fabulis, commessationibus et ebrietatibus,
ceterisque uitae remissioris illecebris subiugatur, et qui magis cotidie uentrem
dapibus, quam mentem sacrificiis caelestibus parent' ('who are given to laughter, jests, tales, feasting and drunkenness, and the other attractions of a lax life,
and who daily feed the stomach with feasts more than the soul on the heavenly
sacrifice').[93] He added: 'Ceterum si de ebrietate, commessatione, luxuria, et
ceteris huiusmodi contagionibus pari ratione tractare uoluerimus, epistolae

---

[90] Edition and translation from Wulfstan of Winchester, *The Life of St Æthelwold*, pp. 22–24 (cap. 12).
[91] Colker, 'Texts of Jocelyn of Canterbury', p. 426.
[92] Winterbottom and Lapidge, *The Early Lives of St Dunstan*, pp. 35–37 (cap. 10).
[93] Bede, *Opera Historica*, vol. I, p. 407.

modus in immensum extenderetur' ('If we wished to deal similarly with drunkenness, feasting, loose living, and other pollutions of this kind, the length of this letter would be immoderately extended').[94]

Alcuin urged his correspondents to be continent in their eating and drinking, to attend to God rather than to players and entertainers, and to foster the *caritas* of selfless brotherhood rather than the *caritas quae in pleno potatur calice* ('the comradeship which is consumed in the full cup'), which obviously held some attraction for his correspondents.[95] To secular interests, by contrast, feasting was an important part of celebration and commemoration. King Æthelstan left fifty hides to the Old Minster in Winchester so that the monks could celebrate an annual feast of three days' length at All Saints' Day in his honour.[96]

Although it is clear that feasting and carousing were the favoured occupations of men in both the secular and the clerical world, the extent to which women caroused as equals at these feasts is uncertain. Archaeological evidence from graves on the Continent suggests that in those areas, at least, women were buried with drinking vessels at a rate on par with men, and some Anglo-Saxon women's graves also contain drinking horns, though whether the women were partaking as often as they were serving is unclear.[97] Women may have been the ones doing the brewing, as they commonly did in later medieval England. The literature does show women present at the feasts, but the most important implication of these passages is again that the women were serving rather than being served. It is unclear what the arrangements might have been when the highest-status drinker was a woman, as may have been the case in the famous *gebeorscipe*s in which Cædmon was asked to sing, in Hild's monastery, as described by Bede.[98] At the consecration of King Edgar in 973, the queen had a separate feast with the abbots and abbesses, though the reason is not clear.[99] There are few specific mentions of women themselves actually drinking. One is the disapproving passage from Ælfric, about women holding their clandestine *gebeorscipe*s in the latrines. Another comes in Riddle 12 of the Exeter Book, which describes a Welsh maiden as 'dol druncmennen' ('a befuddled drunken maidservant'). These references, though small in number, portray women's drinking as illicit and undesirable; but they also suggest that women partook when they could, however censured they might have been.

[94] Bede, *Opera Historica*, vol. I, p. 423.
[95] *Alcuini Epistolae* no. 281 (MGH Epist. 4, pp. 439–40), no. 175 (pp. 190–91), and no. 117 (p. 172), in Dümmler, *Epistolae Karolini Aevi II*.
[96] Robertson, *Anglo-Saxon Charters*, pp. 48–50 at 50 (no. XXV).
[97] Bullough, *Friends, Neighbours and Fellow-drinkers*, pp. 6–7; De Vegvar, 'Beyond Valkyries'.
[98] Bede, *Bede's Ecclesiastical History*, ed. Colgrave and Mynors, pp. 414–17 (iv.24). The Latin is *in conuiuio*; the term *gebeorscipe* is used in the Old English translation.
[99] Byrhtferth of Ramsay, *The Lives of St Oswald and St Ecgwine*, pp. 110–11 (Part 4.7).

The degree to which the English relished feasting left them vulnerable to charges that their indulgent ways were to blame for political calamities. Wulfstan famously blamed the Viking incursions on the sins of the people, among which 'overfilling' – greed in eating and drinking – figured prominently: 'þurh fulne eac folces gælsan ⁊ þurh oferfylla ⁊ mænigfealde synna heora eard hy forworhtan ⁊ selfe hy forwurdan'[100] ('Also through the foul extravagance of the people and through overfilling and manifold sins they wronged their land and they themselves perished'). William of Malmesbury espoused a similar anti-English explanation for the English loss at Hastings. Describing the eve of the battle, he spelled out the contrast between the dissolute English and the pious Normans:

> Ita utrimque animosi duces disponunt aties, patrio quisque ritu. Angli, ut accepimus, totam noctem insomnem cantibus potibusque ducentes … . Contra Normanni, nocte tota confessioni peccatorum uacantes, mane Dominico corpori communicarunt.

> (So the leaders on both sides, in high spirits, drew up their lines of battle, each in the traditional manner. The English – so I have heard – spent a sleepless night in song and wassail …. The Normans on the other hand spent the whole night confessing their sins, and in the morning made their communion.)[101]

Elsewhere, he described the Anglo-Saxons as dissolute and immoral in numerous ways, drunkenness among them:

> Potabatur in commune ab omnibus, in hoc studio noctes perinde ut dies perpetuantibus … . Sequebantur uitia ebrietatis sotia, quae uirorum animos effeminant. Hinc factum est ut, magis temeritate et furore precipiti quam scientia militari Willelmo congressi, uno prelio et ipso perfacili seruituti se patriamque pessumdederint … Ad summam, tunc erant Angli uestibus ad medium genu expediti, crines tonsi, barbas rasi, armillis aureis brachia onerati, picturatis stigmatibus cutem insigniti; in cibis urgentes crapulam, in potibus irritantes uomicam.

> (Drinking in company was a universal practice, and in this passion they made no distinction between night and day. There followed the vices that keep company with drunkenness, and sap the virility of a man's spirit. As a result there was more rashness and headlong fury than military skill in their conflict with William, so that in one battle – and a very easy one – they abandoned themselves and their country to servitude …. In brief, the English of those days wore garments half way to the knee, which left them unimpeded; hair short, chin shaven, arms loaded with gold bracelets, skin tattooed with coloured patterns, eating till they were sick and drinking till they spewed.)[102]

---

[100] Wulfstan, *Sermo Lupi ad Anglos*, p. 66, lines 93–94.

[101] William of Malmesbury, *Gesta Regum Anglorum*, vol. I, pp. 452–54 (cap. 241–42). The charge was repeated elsewhere, for example by Wace, *Le Roman de Rou de Wace*, vol. II, p. 3, ll. 7323–37.

[102] William of Malmesbury, *Gesta Regum Anglorum*, vol. I, pp. 458–59 (Book III, cap. 245.4–5).

Although critics dismissed excessive carousing as a sign of moral weakness, it is clear that feasting and drinking held meaning for the Anglo-Saxons. At a time when hunger was a real threat to many, these activities provided the opportunity for displays of abundance and hierarchy, for celebration and commemoration, and for fellowship and community. And although feasting and carousing demonstrated the power of the elite to commandeer the resources of their supporters, the less powerful also seized the opportunity, when they could, to enjoy such pleasures.

4 Music, Dance, and Performance

> Longað þonne þy læs   þe him con leoþa worn,
> oþþe mid hondum con   hearpan gretan;
> hafaþ him his gliwes giefe,   þe him god sealde.
> — *Maxims I*, 169–71

> (He languishes less who knows an abundance of songs,
> or with his hands can play the harp;
> he has the gift of his playing that God gave him.)

In both the secular realm and the realm of religion, music formed the backdrop of much that happened in Anglo-Saxon culture. In the secular realm, music accompanied dance and overlapped so closely with poetry that the two are difficult to separate. In the realm of religion, music was as an essential part of ecclesiastical life, so much so that Ælfric listed a 'sang-boc', a music book, among the few books with which every priest should be equipped.[103] The status of music as an essential of the church may have elevated its official estimation, and the *scop* or bard was traditionally held in high regard, but some types of musicians and other performers had a seedier reputation, as did the dancing that their music often fostered.

The vast majority of scholarship on Anglo-Saxon music has focused on ecclesiastical music, for the simple reason that evidence survives in abundance, whereas the evidence pertaining to secular music is meagre.[104] Church music was no doubt often pleasurable to listen to, and with its range of sophisticated instruments and techniques, such as organs and polyphony, inspiring and impressive, but it does not really belong in the realm of entertainment and so will not be the focus of this section.

The idea that music was related to the divine underlay much thought about music, secular as well as ecclesiastical. The quote from *Maxims I* that forms the epigraph for this section shows that playing music was regarded as a gift from

---

[103] Ælfric, *Die Hirtenbriefe Ælfrics*, p. 126 (no. 157).

[104] For an overview of Anglo-Saxon music, principally ecclesiastical, see Caldwell, *The Oxford History of English Music*, pp. 1–23.

God. In *The Phoenix*, the narrator uses a comparison with the beauty of music to express the beauty of the song of the phoenix:

> Biþ þæs hleoðres sweg
> eallum songcræftum   swetra ond wlitigra
> ond wynsumra   wrenca gehwylcum.
> Ne magon þam breahtme   byman ne hornas,
> ne heorpan hlyn,   ne hæleþa stefn
> ænges on eorþan,   ne organan,
> sweghleoþres geswin,   ne swanes feðre,
> ne ænig þara dreama   þe dryhten gescop
> gumum to gliwe   in þas geomran woruld. (134–39)

('The sound of [its] song is sweeter and more lovely than all singing and more joyful than every melody. Neither trumpets nor horns, nor the resounding of the harp, nor the voice of men in any way on earth, nor organs, nor the sound of melody, nor the swan's feathers, nor any of the joys that the Lord created as enjoyment for men in this sorrowful world, can exceed its melody.')

Thus, although individual musicians and kinds of music may have had disreputable associations, the potential of music to reach for the divine was also always present.

The extent and character of secular music can probably be assessed to some extent by considering the range of instruments possessed by the Anglo-Saxons. These include harps, lyres, psalteries, fiddles, pipes, horns and trumpets, bagpipes, bells, clappers, drums, and Jew's harps.[105] The highest status was accorded to the harp and the lyre, both of which went under the Old English name *hearpe*. The lyre had a rounded top and parallel sides; the harp was triangular (or just possibly, in some cases, quadrangular), though small rather than large like a modern concert harp. The harp had the imprimatur of the Biblical King David, and the lyre was the favoured instrument of the storytelling *scop* in the hall.[106] The trope of harp music at the hall feast represented joy and merriment, and is found in numerous texts. *Beowulf* put it in its simplest terms, describing the conjunction of feasting, music, and merriment:

> . . . ond we to symble   geseten hæfdon.
> Þær wæs gidd ond gleo. (2104–05)

('And we sat down to the feast. There was song and playing').

---

[105] The most comprehensive overview of Anglo-Saxon musical instruments is Benko, 'Anglo-Saxon Musical Instruments'.

[106] On the *hearpe*, see Boenig, 'The Anglo-Saxon Harp' and Page, 'Anglo-Saxon *Hearpan*'. Because the same term was used for both instruments and certain knowledge of which one is intended is not possible, I have translated *hearpe* as *harp* throughout.

Elsewhere in the poem the harp is called by the poetic term *gomenwudu* (play-wood, joy-wood) (line 1065). The harp was so central to the idea of music that, as Robert Boenig has noted, where the Latin version of Bede's account of Caedmon's hymn has the term 'cantare', the Old English version has translated it as 'be hearpan singan', 'almost as if "to sing" for the Anglo-Saxons was equivalent to "sing with the harp"'.[107]

In the kind of musical storytelling described at several points in *Beowulf* and other works, the lyre appears as the standard instrument accompanying the epics performed in the hall. A passage from *Christ II* summarises the powers of the hall singer, leading into the passage with a description of the wise wordsmith:

> Sumum wordlaþe   wise sendeð
> on his modes gemynd   þurh his muþes gæst,
> æðele ondgiet.   Se mæg eal fela
> singan ond secgan   þam bið snyttru cræft
> bifolen on ferðe.   Sum mæg fingrum wel
> hlude fore hæleþum   hearpan stirgan,
> gleobeam gretan. (665–70)

> (To one he sends wise speech, into the thought of his mind through the breath of his mouth, noble understanding. He may sing and speak of many things, he to whom wise skill is commended in his soul. One may play the harp well, touch the playing-wood, with his fingers, resounding before the warriors.)

What is not clear is the manner of 'singing and speaking' many things, particularly as performed by the harper in the hall: whether the harp music was accompanied by speaking, by singing, by chanting, or by some combination is not clear. Nor is it clear whether the singing counts as 'speaking', or whether these represent different modes of delivery used at different times.

Songs of a traditional type must have also been current in the period. Musicologists have divided monophonic song – which presumably accounts for Anglo-Saxon secular music – into several types, including the laisse, the refrain song, the sequence, and the strophic form.[108] Of these only the refrain song can be cautiously identified in Anglo-Saxon secular music, perhaps represented by the vernacular songs (if they were songs) *Deor* and *Wulf and Eadwacer* and Latin pieces such as the *Veni, dilectissime* lyric found in the Cambridge Songs; with its refrain of *et a et o et a et o*, it may have formed a dance song.[109]

---

[107] Boenig, 'The Anglo-Saxon Harp', pp. 299–300.

[108] On these matters, see Butterfield, 'Vernacular Poetry and Music'.

[109] Davidson, 'Erotic "Women's Songs"'.

In the monastic context, the seat of formal education in music theory and liturgy, music was assigned a masculine status, expressed in numerical ratios and the ways in which music was subject to reason.[110] A fundamental text for this understanding was Boethius' *De institutione musica*, which cited Plato in pronouncing that music 'optime moratam' (of the 'highest moral character') should be 'modesta et simplex et mascula nec effeminata nec fera nec varia' ('temperate, simple, and masculine, rather than effeminate, violent, or fickle'), and that the health of the republic depended on music that upheld these virtues and did not descend 'in turpitudinem' ('into promiscuous ways').[111] The urgency of upholding the masculine character of elite music remained a concern for clerics throughout the medieval period. William of Malmesbury described one such cleric, Thomas of Bayeux (Archbishop of York 1070–1100): 'Illud apud clericos quam maxime agere, ut masculam in aecclesia musicam haberent, nec quicquam effeminate defringentes tenero, ut Persius ait, supplantarent uerba palato' ('His major concern for his clerics was that they should maintain a masculine type of music in church, and not give anything an effeminate turn by, in Persius' phrase, tripping up their words against the roof of their delicate mouths').[112] As Elizabeth Eva Leach has noted, 'The vagueness of Boethius' definition of masculinity in music allows later theorists to define as effeminate anything that they want to denigrate, and anything they wish to praise as masculine.'[113] Although ecclesiastical music might slip into effeminate mode through wayward singing, one mode of music was decidedly feminine. Songs such as *Wulf and Eadwacer, Veni, dilectissime, Levis exsurgit zephirus,* and *Nam languens* can be considered examples of *Frauenlieder*, 'women's songs', both a genre and a rare instance of women's voices (though not necessarily women's authorship), in the cultural expression of the time. These examples of 'women's voices' are all either yearning for love or lamenting the absence of their men, and so depict women exclusively as they express emotion in relation to men and sexual relationships. A few works with a male narrator also voice emotions of longing and devotion, but in these the men are also longing for a man, in this case their lord, as in *The Wanderer* and *Deor*. In none of the surviving literature is a man lovelorn for a woman.

The same focus on emotion appears in a second genre of women's voices: women's speeches from classics such as Virgil and Statius, neumed in

---

[110] Leach, 'Music and Masculinity'.

[111] The Latin is from Boethius, *De institutione arithmetrica,* ed. Friedlein, p. 180 (Book I.1); translation from Boethius, *Fundamentals of Music*, p. 4 (Book 1).

[112] William of Malmesbury, *Gesta Pontificum Anglorum*, ed. Winterbottom, Oxford Scholarly Editions Online, cap. 116*.3.

[113] Leach, 'Music and Masculinity', p. 24.

manuscript for musical performance.[114] The most frequently neumed of these was Dido's lament in the *Aeneid*. These neumed speeches may have been sung as school exercises, where women's laments for the dead had long formed a subject of rhetorical study, and this in turn suggests that the women's speeches might be sung by boys.[115] One wonders whether the women's laments in vernacular verse, such as *Wulf and Eadwacer* and *The Wife's Lament*, were always sung by men – which would be an interesting phenomenon in itself – or whether these are evidence of women singing rather than merely songs in women's voices.

Another form of song that was almost certainly present, but which has not survived, is the work song, sung during repetitive activities such as grinding or weaving. These are evidenced in Scandinavian literature, with a version of a grinding song in *Gróttasöngr* and of a weaving song in *Darraðarljóð*, included in chapter 157 of *Njáls Saga*.[116] Some work songs would have sung by men – for instance, sailors' songs and rowers' songs – but grinding and weaving were performed by women and these work songs would have been women's genres. Another genre of song typically sung by women, lullabies, are also likely to have been present, analogous to the famous Welsh example, *Peis Dinogat*, but again no early English examples survive.

Secular song was unquestionably merry and entertaining as well as useful, as the disapproval of clerics demonstrates. Wulfstan reproved clerics for their love of secular music, altering the words of Isaiah 5.12 ('Cithara et lyra et tympanum et tibia et vinum in conviviis vestris, et opus Domini non respicitis', 'You have cithara and lyre and timbrel and flute and wine in your banquets') to 'Hearpe ⁊ pipe ⁊ mistlic gliggamen dremað eow on beorsele'[117] ('Harp and pipe and various kinds of revelry serenade you in the beer hall'). The *Canons of Edgar* further reproves clerics who might be tempted to create music: 'And riht is þæt ænig preost ne beo ealusceop, ne on ænige wisan gliwige mid him sylfum oðrum mannum, ac beo swa his hade gebyrað, wis and woerðfull'[118] ('And it is not right that any priest should be an ale-scop, nor in any way merry among other men, but be as his position requires, wise and virtuous').

Ælfric reiterated the exhortation: addressing clerics, he enjoined: 'Ne ge gligmenn ne beon' ('Do not be minstrels').[119] The words *ealuscop* and *gligmenn* are unlikely to denote professional secular minstrels, which would be an unlikely profession for a cleric who already has a full-time profession; it is more likely that they indicate the practice of entertaining secular music. That clerics might be inclined to do this is interesting in itself; it suggests that a good many

[114] Ziolkowski, 'Women's Lament'.   [115] Ziolkowski, 'Nota Bene', p. 97.
[116] Sveinsson, *Brennu-Njáls saga*; Magnusson and Palsson, *Njals Saga*; Tolley, *Gróttasongr*.
[117] Wulfstan, *Homilies*, p. 217.   [118] Wulfstan, *Wulfstan's Canons of Edgar*, p. 15 (no. 59).
[119] Ælfric, *Die Hirtenbriefe Aelfrics*, p. 216 (Brief III, no. 188).

of them had learned to play instruments (and thus that instruments were widely available), or at least that they had learned secular songs. Perhaps surprisingly, these secular songs might have been learnt in ecclesiastical contexts, as evidenced by the Cambridge Songs manuscript. This manuscript, now Cambridge University Library Gg.5.35, copied at St Augustine's, Canterbury in the eleventh century, contains some eighty-three songs in Latin and German, some with neumes meant to indicate their tune.[120] The songs include religious lyrics, but also love lyrics, comic narratives, political songs, and others, running the gamut of genres. Whether the manuscript served as a classbook, educating monks in Latin, or the repertoire of a professional *gligman*, is not clear, but even if the songs are meant for a *gligman*, such entertainers likely provided entertainment for the monastery, as is well documented in later centuries.[121] As early as the Council of Clofesho in 747, monasteries were being warned against hosting such entertainments, decreeing that bishops should ensure 'ut . . . monasteria . . . non sint ludicrarum artium receptacula, hoc est, poetarum, citharistarum, musicorum, scurrorum' ('that ... monasteries ... do not become vessels of the frivolous arts, that is, of poets, cithara players, musicians, or buffoons').[122]

The music and songs performed by participants after the feast, as depicted in Bede's account of the cowherd Cædmon and his miraculous song, serve as an example of the music that might be practised in monasteries. The story itself is an instance of a circulating folk motif, and cannot be taken as literal truth; and it does not entirely serve as an instance of the 'frivolous arts', as Cædmon's divinely inspired musical contribution is pious rather than secular and frivolous.[123] The character of the other songs sung around the table is not recoverable. Nevertheless, Bede's account suggests that after-dinner monastic music and entertainment was plausible to his audience, and may have been familiar.

The frivolity of their repertoire no doubt contributed to the lowly reputation of travelling musicians; their itinerant nature most likely also contributed. A stranger without social and familial ties in the community would always be the object of suspicion, and it is no accident that several tales told of travelling minstrels operating as spies.[124] The lyre-playing *scop*s in the hall were

[120] Ziolkowski, *The Cambridge Songs*.

[121] Lindenbaum, 'Entertainment in English Monasteries'.

[122] Haddan and Stubbs, *Councils and Ecclesiastical Documents*, vol. III, p. 368 (no. 16).

[123] Lester, 'The Cædmon Story'; Niles, 'Bede's Cædmon'.

[124] These include two legends told in William of Malmesbury's *Gestum Regum Anglorum*, about King Alfred infilitrating the camp of the Danes disguised as a *mimus*, an entertainer, and the infiltration of the camp of King Athelstan by the Viking king Anlaf disguised as an entertainer (*mimus*) with a harp. Geoffrey of Monmouth told the story of Badulf, the brother of the Saxon leader, who pretends to be a harpist to get access to his brother in a besieged city (*Historia*

venerable, but players of other instruments, especially itinerant players, were questionable.[125] Ælfric tells the story of a sacrilegious man who disregarded the Lenten fast and, instead of going to mass, went to the kitchens and began to wolf down food; his sinfulness predictably brought him to the brink of death.[126] He identifies this gluttonous sinner as a *truð*, a clown or entertainer whose stock-in-trade was the trumpet, an instrument so closely associated with the *truð* that the Old English name for the instrument was *truðhorn*. It is telling that the sins of the *truð* were closely allied pleasures: gorging on food and, by trade, indulging in music and frivolity. Both were seen as antithetical to religious solemnity; and both were widely enjoyed, even in the church.

Dance was closely allied with music, to the point that it was effectively impossible to conceive of dance without the accompaniment of music. The music was produced by musical instruments, but often seems to have been merely produced by the singing of the dancers. Dancing might be considered either as the product of holy rejoicing or as suggestive and profane; but in both cases it connoted a state of transport and abandonment.

Objects from the sixth and seventh centuries, including the Sutton Hoo helmet, depict war dances. A constellation of motifs includes figures with bent knees, one foot with the sole upward, wearing helmets with horn-like or bird-like features, holding multiple spears, and other features. These motifs also occur in contemporary figures found on helmet dies and other artefacts from modern Sweden and Demark, suggesting that there was a widespread tradition of war dances across the region, or at the very least a widespread tradition of depicting war dances on helmets and other artefacts.[127] The dance appears to consist of dancers processing in a line, wearing war gear and helmets, sometimes in animal masks, sometimes with a sword in a sword-belt or held aloft, and carrying two spears. In at least one case, the depiction of a warrior on the seventh-century Finglesham buckle, the warrior is conspicuously naked, wearing only a belt and a helmet.[128] The dance itself may have taken place in a line or procession, or among crossed spears laid out on the ground, as may be represented on the Sutton Hoo helmet. Such dances would not have been 'entertainment' in the sense of recreation, but

Regum Britannie ix.1). Geffrai Gaimar's *Estoire des Engleis* also includes the story of a treacherous jester who contributes to the death of Edward the Martyr (lines 3983–96). For more, see Bayless, 'Merriment'.

[125] On the ways the *scop* was associated with venerable antiquity, see Battles and Wright, '*Eall-feala Ealde Sæge*'. On the reputation of musicians, see Breeze, 'The Status of Secular Musicians'.

[126] Ælfric, *Lives of Saints*, pp. 264–65 (no. 12, Ash Wednesday).

[127] For more on all of these topics on dance, see Bayless, 'The Fuller Brooch'.

[128] Hawkes, Davidson, and Hawkes, 'The Finglesham Man'.

would certainly have been stirring and emotive, fostering courage and cohesion, and enjoyable to the participants.[129]

Dances might also be a part of feasting and carousal. The complaint of King Edgar about the pastimes of clerics paints a scenario of drinking and feasting, gaming, singing, dancing, and sexual licence, all apparently in the same evening and late into the night. He described how the clerics 'diffluant in comessationibus et ebrietatibus, in cubilibus et impudicitiis; ut jam domus clericorum putentur prostibula meretricum, conciliabulum histrionum. Ibi aleae, ibi saltus et cantus, ibi usque ad medium noctis spatium protractae in clamore et horrore vigiliae'[130] ('expend themselves in feasting and drinking sessions, in beds and acts of shamelessness; so that now the houses of the clerics are considered brothels of prostitutes, gathering-places for performers. There gaming takes place, there dancing and singing, there people are awake until the middle of the night with loud noise and uncouth behaviour').

There are a number of witnesses as to what such dancing may have looked like. One form of common dance was the chain dance, in which dancers processed, with some kind of hopping or dance steps, in a line, holding hands. In some instances the dancers formed a circle; they might also form a circle without holding hands. The *Vita S. Dunstani*, a product of the 990s, describes a vision of Dunstan in which he peered into a church and saw holy supernatural virgins dancing a round dance, accompanied by a song with a lead and a chorus: 'uidit . . . uirgineas turmas in choro gyranti hymnum hunc poetae Sedulii cursitando cantantes: "Cantemus, socii, Domino" . . . . Itemque perpendit easdem post uersum et uersum uoce reciproca, quasi in circumitionis suae concentu, primum uersiculum eiusdem ymniculi more humanarum uirginum repsallere' ('[he saw that] bands of virgins were wheeling around in a dance, singing as they moved the hymn of Sedulius that begins "Let us sing, friends, to the Lord" . . . . He also noticed that after each verse they alternately repeated, as mortal girls might have done, and as though in harmony with their circling dance, the first couplet of the hymn').[131]

Additional evidence appears in an English version of the 'Dancers of Kolbeck' motif. The story, which circulated both on the Continent and in England, tells of dancers who danced in a churchyard on a holy day and were accursed by being unable to detach their hands from each other or to stop dancing. Among numerous other instances, the story appears in the life of St Edith by Goscelin of Saint-Bertin, composed in England between 1078 and 1087. Goscelin writes, in the voice of the dancer, 'Conserimus manus et chorollam confusionis in atrio ordinamus' ('We join hands and set in motion

---

[129] The capacity for such effects is explored in McNeill, *Keeping Together in Time*.
[130] Birch, *Cartularium Saxonicum*, vol. III, p. 573.
[131] Edition and translation from Winterbottom and Lapidge, *Early Lives*, pp. 100–01 (cap. 36).

our tumultuous dance'), and later describes the dancers as making 'saltus et rotatus' ('hops and spins').[132] Circle dancing in this way, accompanied by a song, seems to have been the standard form of dancing in the later Middle Ages, and the form became known as a carol.[133]

A different, more individual form of dance is also depicted in a number of sources. This is a dance that seems to consist of moving the feet and arms – more specificity is not possible – while either alone or perhaps in a pair. The two dancers depicted in the eighth-century Vespasian Psalter (British Library (BL) Cotton Vespasian A.i, fol. 30v), depicting jubilation before the Lord, seem to be lifting up their feet and clapping. An image in the eleventh-century Harley Psalter (BL Harley 603, fol. 24v) depicts a scene of rejoicing in which a man and a woman dance facing each other, hands in the air, while a second woman dances more sedately to the side, again with her hands in the air; the three dancers are accompanied by five musicians. Another eleventh-century manuscript (BL Claudius B.iv, fol. 92v), depicts the rejoicing at the parting of the Red Sea, and the six figures shown are exulting with their arms held up and their feet in dancing positions, but are not interacting with each other. These examples seem to suggest that dancing could take place without any special configuration, either in pairs or with each person dancing singly.

Contemporary texts make reference to women's erotic dance, conducted by the woman alone, but there is no evidence that such a thing was genuinely a formal category in Anglo-Saxon England. The sin of Lust is personified as a dancing girl in three Anglo-Saxon manuscripts of the *Psychomachia*, all based on Continental prototypes, and the biblical dance of Salome no doubt figured in the depiction of the sinful dancing temptress.[134] The one contemporary account comes from the *Vita* of Wulfstan, bishop of Worcester (c. 1008–1095), first written by Coleman, Wulfstan's chaplain and chancellor, but now surviving only in a Latin version by William of Malmesbury, so its credibility as a first-hand witness is dubious. The *Vita* reports that when young, Wulfstan was engaged in sports on the village green when he was confronted by a dancing seductress: 'puellae predictae quae propter astaret infudit animo ut accurreret. Illa non segnis gestibus impudiciis, motibus inuerecundis, plausabilem psaltriam agit, id ut amasii sui seruiret oculis'[135] ('[The Devil] put it into the mind of the aforesaid girl, who was

---

[132] Wilmart, 'La légende', p. 288; my translation. For more on this motif as it relates to dance, see Bayless, 'Fuller Brooch', pp. 201–02.

[133] Page, 'The Carol?'; Greene, *The Early English Carols*; Mullally, *The Carole*.

[134] The manuscripts are Cambridge, Corpus Christi College 23, fol. 19v; London, British Library, Add. 24199, fol. 18r; and London, British Library, Cotton Cleopatra C.viii, fol. 19v. For more on Anglo-Saxon depictions of sinful dancing girls, all of which are based on religious precedents rather than on contemporary women, see Bayless, 'Fuller Brooch', pp. 196–98.

[135] *Vita Wulfstani*, i.I.6–7, in William of Malmesbury, *Saints' Lives*, p. 18.

standing near, to present herself. She didn't hang about but, to the accompaniment of a harp, began to dance in front of him with lewd gestures and shameless movements such as might gratify the eyes of a lover').[136]

This post-type of Salome, however implausible, is witness to the presence of the 'male gaze', even in the rejecting eye of a would-be saint. In the illustrations of Lust in the *Psychomachia*, as in the *Vita* of Wulfstan, males are depicted gazing at the women in a clearly sexual interaction, although in the instance of Wulfstan the sexual component is blamed squarely on the woman rather than on the man's interpretative gaze. Dunstan's vision in the *Vita S. Dunstani* forms yet another instance, however holy the virgins: they are appealing young women being peered at secretly by a sort of saintly peeping tom. The motif is clearly related to other stories in which men spy on dancing maidens, such as the legend of the Anglo-Saxon nobleman Eadric Wild, who was said to have come across a dwelling of supernaturally beautiful dancing maidens at the edge of a forest. 'Circuibant leui motu gestuque iocundo, et castigata uoce' ('They were circling with lithe motion and merry gesture and with restrained voices'), reported Walter Map.[137] Spying on the maidens, Eadric is inflamed with desire and manages to carry one off despite being bitten and scratched by the others. In the end, it seems that the alluring dance was a trap to ensnare him into marriage with a demonic wife, a worry that might have motivated a number of contemporary men who deplored the seductive wiles of dancing women. The only surviving instances of the Old English terms for 'female dancer', *sealticge*, *hleapestre*, and *hoppestre*, are in a pejorative context, each used to refer to Salome, who asked for the head of John the Baptist as a reward for her dancing (Matthew 14.6–11, Mark 6.21–28).[138] It may be that less condemnatory uses of the terms simply did not make it into the surviving written record, or that the Old English terms were coined solely for these instances, but the terms do support a pattern that distinguished female dancers for their seductive qualities, and that repeatedly depicted men peeping at them.

A few additional varieties of dance have left the scantest evidence. There may have been a kind of satirical dance, as was attested more widely in Scandinavian sources where they were called *dansa*, a dance to satirical songs.[139] The sole evidence remaining from England is in a complaint of Edgar about the depravity of the clergy: he charged that such abuses were so infamous that 'Haec milites

---

[136] Translation by Swanton, *Three Lives*, p. 94.

[137] Map, *De nugis curialium*, p. 154 (dist. ii, c. 12).

[138] The terms *sealicge* and *hleapestre* appear (in the accusative) in the description of Salome in Rauer, *The Old English Martyrology*, pp. 170–71; *hoppestre* appears in a description of Salome in Ælfric, *Ælfric's Catholic Homilies: The First Series*, p. 455 (no. XXXII, line 121).

[139] For more on this, see Bayless, 'Fuller Brooch', p. 206.

clamant, plebs submurmurat, mimi cantant et saltant' ('Soldiers shout about these things, people mutter them, performers sing and dance about them').[140] This would be a rare glimpse at dance as social satire, as well as at the presence of professional performers, who are otherwise effectively absent from the records.

Secular ceremonial dance is suggested by the traditional horn dance still conducted in the village of Abbots Bromley, Staffordshire, where one of the reindeer horns used in the dance has been calculated as having a 95 per cent chance of dating from between 998 and 1269 (see Section 7). This is one of the few Anglo-Saxon dance traditions (if it was indeed a dance tradition) that can be firmly connected to a specific occasion, and suggests that other celebrations may also have been enlivened by dance. On the Continent there is abundant evidence of dance traditions accompanying festivals, conducted in streets or churchyards, and sometimes involving dressing as stags or wearing other disguises.[141] Although virtually no evidence of such traditions survives from England until the later period, it would be unsurprising to find that the Anglo-Saxons enjoyed themselves in such ways as heartily as their Continental cousins.

Music was obviously part of the range of performed entertainment in Anglo-Saxon England, both by itself and in conjunction with storytelling. The question of the overall scope of performance is a vexed one, however, with partial and inconclusive evidence.[142] Old English has a number of terms for entertainers and performers, including *scop* (bard), *gligman/gleoman/gliwere* (player/performer/musician), *leasere* (performer/actor, literally a 'liar'), *spillere* (player, perhaps a jester), *truð* (buffoon), *tumbere* (tumbler, dancer, acrobat), *fæðel* (player), *scericge* (actress), and perhaps *þyle* (orator) and *woþbora* (orator). The differences between all these performers is not clear.[143] A number of these terms occur primarily as glosses on Latin texts that reflect the practices of other cultures, so it is not even clear whether all of these were the standard names for English performers. The same is true of most references to theatre, which occur in reference to Latin texts and practices of other cultures rather than serving as evidence of anything like theatre in Anglo-Saxon England.[144] Much drama in medieval Europe seems to have

---

[140] Birch (ed.), *Cartularium Saxonicum*, vol. III, pp. 572–73.

[141] For more on the abundant evidence for these traditions on the Continent, see Filotas, *Pagan Survivals*, pp. 154–82 and Barillari, 'Le maschere cornute', pp. 529–48.

[142] The larger contemporary context for English performers is given by Ogilvy, '*Mimi, Scurrae, Histriones*'.

[143] The vocabulary for Anglo-Saxon performers, singers, and poets, including the complex questions of Latin terms and evidence from glossaries, is discussed by Opland, *Anglo-Saxon Oral Poetry*, pp. 230–56; Thornbury, *Becoming a Poet*, pp. 14–36; and Bayless, 'Merriment'.

[144] These references are explored in Tydeman et al., *The Medieval European Stage*, pp. 27–30 and Price, 'Theatrical Vocabulary (1)' and 'Theatrical Vocabulary (2)'.

arisen out of religious enactments of biblical episodes, and it has been argued that liturgical drama first arose from the *Quem quaeritis* trope of Easter matins, in which different clerics read out the dialogue between the angels and the women at the tomb of Jesus, as implied in Luke 24.[145]

Other kinds of performance must have taken place in a variety of settings: in the halls of the mighty, in humbler houses, and on street and other occasions such as fairs and festivals. Two pieces of possible structural evidence exist. The palace of Edwin, a seventh-century king of Northumbria, at Yeavering, included a 'theatre' or grandstand, with a platform from which one man could address others or perform for them. When Edwin inherited the 'theatre' it was large enough for around 120 people, but he expanded it to hold around 320. This may merely have served for governmental or ecclesiastical assemblies, but there is also the possibility that performances could have been held there. As one scholar has described it: 'The small size of its dais and the form of its 'arena' do not allow of its having been designed or used for spectacle or drama in the classical sense. Evidently it was contrived to focus the attention of a large concourse primarily on a single individual standing, or more probably sitting, in front of Post E.'[146] The dais may be what is meant by a gloss on *orcista uel pulpitus*: 'gligmanna yppe' ('performers' platform').[147]

Whether situated on a platform or not, some performances must have had the impact of 'shows'. A further piece of testimony about open-air performance was given by two texts that describe the practice of Aldhelm, who enticed people into religion by setting up as an open-air singer. In the description by William of Malmesbury:

> Populum eo tempore semibarbarum, parum diuinis sermonibus intentum, statim cantatis missis, domos cursitare solitum. Ideo sanctum virum, super pontem qui rura et urbem continuat, abeuntibus se opposuisse obicem, quasi artem cantitandi professum. Eo plusquam semel facto, plebis fauorem et concursum emeritum. Hoc commento sensim inter ludicra uerbis scripturarum insertis, ciues ad sanitatem reduxisse.

> (The people of his day were more or less barbarians, who paid little heed to the word of God, and were prone to run off home immediately after the singing of mass. So the holy man took his stand on the bridge that links city and country and barred their way, playing the part of a professional minstrel. After he had done this more than once, the common people were won over and flocked to listen to him. Exploiting this device, he gradually started to

---

[145] See, for instance, Petersen, 'Les textes polyvalents' and Bedingfield, *The Dramatic Liturgy*, pp. 160–65.

[146] Hope-Taylor, *Yeavering*, p. 161.   [147] Kindschi, 'The Latin-Old English Glossaries'.

smuggle words from the Scriptures into the less serious matter, and so brought the inhabitants round to sound sentiments.)[148]

The description of Aldhelm's minstrelsy comes some 400 years after his time, though it comes from Aldhelm's own monastery, so it is not impossible that it preserves a genuine account. At the least, it can be said that in the late eleventh century it was plausible that a minstrel should play in a thoroughfare of the city. The *scop*, perhaps best translated 'bard', is known principally from romantic depictions of the elite hall feast. The *gligman, gleoman*, or *gliwere*, by contrast, seems to have been a more versatile performer. In *Widsith* the performer travels widely, but other evidence suggests that entertainers might be attached to courts or in the service of lords. Glosses link *gleoman* with *parasitus* ('retainer').[149] Elsewhere, the terms *circulator, seductor* ('peddler, seducer/charlatan') are glossed *gligmann*, which certainly does not speak to a high status on the part of the *gligmann*.[150]

A striking aspect of the performers mentioned in Anglo-Saxon sources is that in nearly all cases music formed part of the performance. People must have told stories without the accompaniment of music, but as an art form even storytelling is not attested without the accompaniment of the harp. The presence of music even holds true for performances that might well have forgone music, such as juggling. In the Tiberius Psalter (BL Cotton Tiberius C. VI, fol. 30 v, produced in eleventh-century Winchester), King David plays a triangular harp accompanied by a fiddler, a musician playing a pipe, another playing a horn, and a juggler juggling three balls and three knives. An image in Trinity College, Cambridge (B.5.26, fol. 1r, produced in Canterbury 1070 x 1100) similarly shows David playing a triangular harp, accompanied by a musician playing a fiddle and a juggler juggling three knives.[151] In 2 Samuel 6:5, David and all Israel are described playing before the Lord, 'citharis et lyris et tympanis et sistris et cymbalis' ('on harps and lutes and timbrels and cornets and cymbals'), but nothing is said about jugglers. These images show that additional merriment might even be smuggled into scripture, as it was into the everyday life of Anglo-Saxons, secular and religious alike.

---

[148] William of Malmesbury, *Gesta Pontificum Anglorum*, ed. and trans. Thomson and Winterbottom, vol. II, pp. 506–07 (Book V cap. 190.4.) The incident is also recounted in the late-eleventh-century *Vita S. Aldhelmi* of Faricius, a monk at Malmesbury; one edition is Winterbottom, 'An Edition of Faricius', with the incident at p. 102 (cap. 5.4).

[149] Goossens, *The Old English Glosses*, p. 412.

[150] Meritt, *The Old English Prudentius Glosses*, p. 47.

[151] On jugglers of this period, see Fletcher, 'Jugglers Celtic and Anglo-Saxon'. Fletcher proposes that similarities between Anglo-Saxon and Celtic juggling, such as the use of both balls and knives, may suggest links between the two traditions.

5 The Pleasures of Literature

> Hwilum cyninges þegn,
> guma gilphlæden,   gidda gemyndig,
> se ðe ealfela   ealdgesegena
> worn gemunde,   word oþer fand
> soðe gebunden;   secg eft ongan
> sið Beowulfes   snyttrum styrian,
> ond on sped wrecan   spel gerade,
> wordum wrixlan . . . .
>
> —*Bewoulf* 867–74

> (At times the king's thane, a glory-skilled
> man, calling songs to mind – he who knew
> a great many old sagas – devised a new tale,
> bound together well; again the man began to
> recite Beowulf's journey with craft and to tell
> the tale skilfully and with discernment, vary-
> ing his words.)

The term 'literature' is not fully suitable for the focus of this section, being conventionally used for work that is written on the page, which in the Anglo-Saxon period formed a minority of the circulating works of verbal artistry. The word *orature* has been coined to denote oral works; but even if one accepts this rather ungainly term, neither were Anglo-Saxon works wholly oral. Although there is no convenient and precise term to encompass the spectrum of verbal works created for enjoyment, this section will cover them all: written, spoken, and sung.

Such works were not just an individual pleasure, but a vital part of community in Anglo-Saxon England. Storytelling and poetry were bearers of culture, forming networks of meaning, providing connection, reflection, wisdom, encouragement, solace, and delight. Surviving works tend to be sombre: reflective, such as *The Wanderer* and *The Seafarer*; expressions of emotion, sometimes consolatory and sometimes not, such as *Wulf and Eadwacer* or *Deor*; religious narrative, such as the verse *Genesis* or Ælfric's *Lives of Saints*; wisdom-oriented, such as *Maxims*, *The Gifts of Men*, and *The Fates of Men*; historical or political, such as Bede's *Ecclesiastical History*, *The Battle of Maldon*, or the celebratory poems found in the Anglo-Saxon Chronicle; or informational, such as *The Rune Poem*, *The Seasons for Fasting*, and even the charms. A less directly utilitarian genre is what might be called wonder texts, which includes *Beowulf*, *The Wonders of the East*, *The Letter of Alexander to Aristotle*, *Widsith*, many of the riddles, and works such as Aldhelm's *Carmen Rhythmicum*, which describes a powerful storm. But even the more pedagogical of these texts show literary sensibilities and, often, a playful creativity. The prose *Solomon and*

Saturn dialogue on the qualities of the Pater Noster, for instance, is extravagantly imaginative:

> Saturnus cwæð, 'Ac hulic heafod hafað se Pater Noster?'
> Salomon cwæð, 'Pater Noster hafað gylden heafod and sylfren feax, and ðeah ðe ealle eorðan wæter sien gemenged wið ðam heofonlicum wætrum uppe on ane ædran, ond hit samlice rinan onginne eall middangerd, mid eallum his gesceaftum, he mæg under ðæs Pater Nosters feaxe anum locce drige gestandan.'[152]

> (Saturn said: 'And what kind of head does the Pater Noster have?'
> Solomon said: 'The Pater Noster has a golden head and silver hair, and even if all the waters of the earth were mingled together with the heavenly waters up high in a single stream and it began to rain at the same time, all earth together with all its created things could stand dry under one lock of the hair of the Pater Noster.')

Playful too are many of the first-person and self-referential inscriptions on objects, such as the 'whalebone' riddle on the Franks Casket, of which the answer is the casket itself.[153] The artistry and imagination that went into such verbal works show that not only did the Anglo-Saxons aim to learn from their literature, they also aimed to enjoy it.[154]

The most prominent and perhaps the highest-status form of literature was poetry, whether alliterative (or, occasionally, rhymed) Old English metrical verse or metrical Latin poetry.[155] The status of verse was only magnified by the inheritance of the Classical poets and the long Latin tradition of composing verse versions of prose texts. In Anglo-Saxon England this took the form, for example, of Aldhelm's prose *De virginitate* and verse *De virginitate* or Bede's two *Lives* of St Cuthbert, one in prose and one in verse. The same impulse produced versified versions of sections of the Bible such as *Genesis* and *Exodus* and verse accounts of biblical figures such as *Andreas* and *Elene*, and of course *Christ*.

Much of this poetry must have been intended to be heard communally, but poetry was also appreciated privately. Alcuin's many poems sent to correspondents evince a sheer love of versifying. And although much of the circulating Latin poetry had a spiritual aim, it could also be playful. The verse epistle from Herbert to Wulfgar, Abbot of Abingdon (990–1016), describing the harshness of winter and begging for

---

[152] Edited in Anlezark, *The Old English Dialogues.*

[153] On first-person inscriptions, see Paz, *Nonhuman Voices.*

[154] The functions of traditional literature are addressed in Niles, *Homo Narrans.* Niles analyses the functions as ludic, sapiential (transmitting wisdom), normative (reflecting and establishing norms), constitutive (delineating basic cultural categories), socially cohesive (promoting community), and adaptive (processing cultural change). Although Niles focuses on oral poetry, these categories would apply to any form of traditional, culturally important literature. As he points out, none of these secondary elements is possible unless the text is ludic, because no one will be attentive to the other elements if the text does not entertain them.

[155] On Anglo-Saxon poetry, and poets generally, see Thornbury, *Becoming a Poet.*

a cloak, embodies this playfulness. Complaining about the winter, Herbert laments that the cold is worse to the tonsured:

> Multi plorabunt lacrimis sine sorte doloris;
>   In naribus certe guttula pendet aquę.
> Omnibus et caluis aderit tunc maxima pestis;
>   Inuadent caluos frigora, nix, pluuia.

> ('Though not bereaved, many then will weep with tears.
> And drops of water will surely hang from noses!
> Winter is then a great plague especially to the bald.
> Chilling cold, snow, and rain attack the bare of pate!')[156]

The brusque verse reply from Wulfgar, denying the request, could be regarded as sardonic; or it could merely be withering.

Verse was also used for the otherwise pedestrian aims of delineating the times for fasting (*The Seasons for Fasting*) and laying out the calendar of religious festivals (*The Menologium*): the verse form gave the information formality, authority, and memorability.

On the less elite level, it is clear that charms too were thought to be more powerful when composed in verse and spoken aloud. Verse cast a spell, literally and metaphorically.

It is not wholly clear how poetry such as *Genesis*, *Elene*, or the poetic *Life* of St Cuthbert was experienced. The texts may have been read for private devotion, but the likelihood is that they were read aloud in monasteries, perhaps during meals. Communal monastic literature was reportedly not restricted to religious texts, however. Alcuin's famous complaint paints a picture of monastic entertainment: 'Ibi decet lectorem audiri, non citharistam; sermones patrum, non carmina gentilium. Quid Hinieldus cum Christo?'[157] ('It is fitting to listen to a reader, not a cithara-player; to the sayings of the Fathers, not the verses of the pagans. What does Ingeld have to do with Christ?').

The passage demonstrates both that secular narratives might form the entertainment in monasteries and that such narratives were experienced communally. It is not clear if we should imagine a performer or monk reciting the tales of Ingeld aloud while the monks are eating, or whether an *ealu-scop*, either a secular performer or one of the monks, is performing the tales to the accompaniment of the harp after dinner, as might happen in a secular hall.[158] However it was delivered,

---

[156] Porter, 'The Anglo-Latin Elegy', pp. 240, 243 (lines 23–26).

[157] From the letter to 'Speratus', edited by Dümmler, *Epistolae Karolini Aevi*, vol. II, p. 183 (no. 124).

[158] The scholarship on *scops*, bards, oral composition, and the issues of literacy is immense. Among the important studies on the topic are O'Keeffe, *Visible Song*; Frank, 'The Search for the Anglo-Saxon Oral Poet'; Pasternak, *The Textuality of Old English Poetry*; and Niles, 'The Myth of the Anglo-Saxon Poet'.

such fare apparently formed part of monastic entertainment in the eighth century, when Alcuin voiced his complaint, and religious taste remained similarly wide in the eleventh century, when the monks of St Augustine's, Canterbury copied out the Cambridge Songs manuscript with its range of secular songs, which may have formed the libretto for many evenings of communal entertainment.

The delivery of secular poetry is even less certain. Old English verse epics are depicted as being 'told' in the hall, though whether this means they were sung, chanted, spoken to music, or otherwise, remains obscure. As Robert Boenig has noted, the description of the *scop*'s performance in *Beowulf* is poised between music and speech: 'What we learn of the harp in this passage is that it is played in a loud and mirthful hall and that it accompanies a poetic rendition, which, surprisingly, is invested with verbs of speaking rather than singing (*sægde, reccan, cwæð*), although the performance is called a *sang*.'[159] Whatever the precise manner of delivery, this kind of literature was experienced aloud and communally. This was, so to speak, the default mode for vernacular literature, and could be true even when written texts were involved. Asser's *Life* of King Alfred depicts the king reading vernacular texts, but aloud and with an eye towards memorisation. He classed the king's literary efforts among his other laudatory practices, including governing, hunting, and directing elite craftsmen, and praised his determination 'Saxonicos libros recitare, et maxime carmina Saxonica memoriter discere' ('reading aloud from books in English and above all learning English poems by heart').[160] The Old English riddles paint a similar picture of literature experienced 'out loud', as in riddle 42, which says that the answer must be guessed by 'werum æt wine' ('men at wine').[161]

The Anglo-Saxon love of narrative is apparent from the many narrative poems, and arguably also from narratives such as saints' lives; although the purpose of these was ostensibly spiritual inspiration, their drama and incident must have appealed to the imagination as well. This would have been particularly true of the saints' lives that came very close to folktale, such as the legends of St Kenelm and St Mildrith, or to romance, such as the legends of Eustace. Some narratives, such as Bede's story of Cædmon's miraculous verse-making, came straight from the world of folktales.[162]

---

[159] Boenig, 'The Anglo-Saxon Harp', p. 292.

[160] Asser, *Asser's Life of King Alfred*, p. 59 (cap. 76); translation from Keynes and Lapidge, *Alfred the Great*, p. 91.

[161] Krapp and Dobbie, *The Exeter Book*, no. 42.

[162] As many as forty-five analogues to the Cædmon story have been proposed; however many of these are accounted valid, it is clear that the motif was taken from folklore tradition. Among the scholarship on this is Lester, 'The Cædmon Story' and Niles, 'Bede's Cædmon'. On the folklore components of other Anglo-Saxon religious narrative, see, for instance, Cubitt, 'Folklore and Historiography' and Powell, '"Once Upon a Time There Was a Saint"'.

It is not clear whether secular narrative prose existed as a formal genre, but tales certainly existed and were passed down through the centuries, gathering incident as they grew.[163] Legends of the evil queen Cwoenthrith/Quendrida and later of the death of Edward the Martyr appeared in multiple forms, reflecting ongoing transmission, probably both oral and written.[164] Longer narratives, very possibly in prose, are also implied by some of the short verse works that would probably have had a backstory, such as *Wulf and Eadwacer* or *The Wife's Lament*. These are very like the short poems expressing emotion that appear in prose narratives in Wales and Ireland, as well as resembling the Latin prosimetrum form found in texts like the *Consolation of Philosophy*, so it is not difficult to imagine that these represent a tradition of prose narratives punctuated by poems that existed in Anglo-Saxon England as well. Whether prose tales, with or without poetic or song interludes, would have been narrated by the·*scop*, by the *gligman*, or by a professional of another name is not clear.

The Anglo-Saxon love of plot also surfaces in other genres. The *Maxims* poems, for instance, might be categorised as rosters of narrative elements: the king rules the kingdom, the lord gives out rings, the monster lurks alone in the fen, the dragon hoards gold, and the young woman involves herself in a plot:

> Ides sceal dyrne cræfte,
> fæmne hire freond gesecean,   gif heo nelle on folce geþeon
> þæt hi man beagum gebicge.[165]

('A maiden shall with secret cunning seek out her lover, if she does not want to flourish among her people in order that a man may buy her with rings').

The pleasures of plot and poetry can also be found embedded in the Anglo-Saxon Chronicle. The entry for 1003, as found in the C, D, and E versions, depicts a historical event that has already begun to evolve into legend, with sensationalist motifs, a proverb, and a suggestion of verse:

> Ða sceolde se ealdorman Ælfric lædan þa fyrde, ac he teah forð þa his ealdan wrenceas. Sona swa hi wæron swa gehende þet ægðer heora on oðer hawede, þa gebræd he hine seocne and ongan hine brecan to spiwenne and cweð þet he gesiclod wære and swa þet folc beswac þet he lædan sceolde swa hit gecweðen is: ðonne se heretoga wacað, þonne bið eall se here swiðe gehindred. Ða Swegen geseah þet hi anræde næron and ealle tohwurfon, þa lædde he his here into Wiltune, and hi ða burh gehergodon and forbærndon and eodon þa to Searbyrig, and þanon eft to sæ ferde þær he wiste his yðhengestas.[166]

---

[163] These narratives been most throughly explored by Wright, *The Cultivation of Saga*.
[164] An orientation to the versions is provided by Wright, *The Cultivation of Saga*, pp. 99–104, 161–71.
[165] Dobbie, *The Anglo-Saxon Minor Poems*, pp. 56–57 (lines 43–45).
[166] Irvine, *The Anglo-Saxon Chronicle*, s.v. 1003, p. 64.

(Then the ealdorman Ælfric should have led the forces, but he pulled out his old tricks. As soon as they were close enough that each [army] could look on the other, then he pretended to be sick and began to vomit, and said that he was sick, and so betrayed the people that he should have led. Thus it is said, 'When the leader is weak, the whole army is greatly impeded.' When Sweyn saw that they were not of one mind and all broken up, then he led his army into Wilton. And they ravaged and burned the city, and went to Salisbury and from there again he went to sea where he knew his wave-stallions [ships] were.)

The charge that the vomiting leader was feigning, the implication that there were prior stories of 'old tricks', the proverb, the kenning *yðhengestas*, and the fact that the passage can be read metrically – all are signs of literature emerging out of documentation.[167]

Literary motifs and concerns are found in other unlikely corners of the written record. The legend of Cynewulf and Cyneheard, inscribed under the year 755 in the Anglo-Saxon Chronicle, has become celebrated for its compressed yet still dramatic story of the developing feud between the kinsmen Cynewulf and Cyneheard.[168] As one scholar has observed, 'The story is self-contained, lively and dramatic, with a faint touch of sex, and a good deal of violence.'[169] This interest in the dramatic power of feuds between relatives also makes an appearance in the question-and-answer dialogue *Adrian and Ritheus*. The item turns on the belief that, after snakes mate, the female kills the male and then the offspring kill the mother by bursting out of her. The author has framed this in feuding terms:

Saga me hwilc sunu wræce his fæder on hys moder innoðe.
Ic þe secge, þære næddran sunu, for þam ðe seo moder ofsloh ær þane fæder, and þonne ofsleað þa bearn eft þa moder. [170]

('Tell me which son avenged his father in his mother's innards.'
'I say to thee, the son of the snake, because beforehand the mother slew the father, and then afterwards the children slay the mother.')

Riddles, then, might combine the pleasures of drama, paradox, and the guessing element. The element of paradox that forms the heart of many riddles may also offer the pleasures of metaphor, as in this further item from *Adrian and Ritheus*:

---

[167] On these, see Hill, '"When the Leader Is Brave"'; Bredehoft, 'OE *Yðhengest*'; Weiskott, *English Alliterative Verse*, p. 177 (Appendix A no. 4); and Konshuh, '*Anraed* in their *Unraed*', pp. 155–57. The E version of the Chronicle is edited by Irvine, *The Anglo-Saxon Chronicle*.

[168] The literature on the episode is voluminous, although most studies explore the relevance of the episode for contemporary politics. Relevant articles include McTurk, '"Cynewulf and Cyneheard"'; Heinemann, '"Cynewulf and Cyneheard"'; Wrenn, 'A Saga of the Anglo-Saxons'; and Bremmer, 'The Germanic Context'.

[169] Bremmer, 'The Germanic Context', p. 445.

[170] Cross and Hill, *The Prose Solomon*, p. 36 (*Adrian and Ritheus* no. 12).

Saga me hwilc man wære dead and nære acenned and æfter þam deaðe wære
eft bebyried in his moder innoðe.
Ic þe secge, þæt wæs Adam se æresta man, for þam eorðe wæs his moder and
he wæs bibiriged eft in þære eorðan.[171]

('Tell me which man was dead and was not born, and after death was buried in
his mother's womb.'
'I say to thee, that was Adam the first man, because earth was his mother and
he was buried afterwards in the earth.')

The question-and-answer texts and the riddles represent a genre of interactive
literature, a genre well-represented on the page as well as in the community.
Riddle collections include the Latin verse riddles of Tatwine, Bede, Eusebius, and
Boniface, as well as possibly the anonymous Lorsch riddles; the Latin prose riddles
of Alcuin's *Disputatio Pippini*; and the large collection of Old English verse
riddles.[172] Other kinds of verbal wit were less likely to be recorded. People must
have made jokes, employed sarcasm, and laughed, but what provoked their laughter
rarely made it into the written record. The scholarship on the subject has looked at
verbal incongruity, juxtaposition, and the causes of laughter, but apart from the
obscene Old English riddles and a few passages of Ælfric Bata's *Colloquy*, most of
the humour is subtle at best. The laughter in Anglo-Saxon literature is more often
the expression of noble emotions such as triumph and a disdain for earthly things
rather than of the more common causes of mirth.[173] The verbal wit that is most often
preserved in the written record is sardonic, such as the response to complainers
recorded in the *Durham Proverbs*: "Wide ne biþ wel", cwæþ se þe gehyrde on helle
hriman' ('"Things are bad all over", said he who heard the screaming in hell').[174]

Sophisticated flyting, or exchanges of insults, may have existed as a genre, as it
did in Scandinavia, but the only surviving hints are the string of schoolboy insults in
the *Colloquy* of Ælfric Bata (discussed in Section 2) and possibly the 'Unferth'
episode of *Beowulf*, in which Unferth and Beowulf trade jibes. A few jocular
nicknames have survived in the record, most notably that of Alured Taddebelloc
(Alfred Toad-balls) – though it is hard to imagine how anyone could happen to come
by this nickname – and whatever was the vernacular form of the eleventh-century

171 Cross and Hill, *The Prose Solomon*, p. 38 (*Adrian and Ritheus* no. 28).
172 On these, see, among other works, Orchard, *The Old English and Anglo-Latin Riddle Tradition*;
      Bitterli, *Say What I Am Called*; and Bayless, 'Alcuin's *Disputatio Pippini*'.
173 Old English laughter is examined by Tucker, 'Laughter in Old English Literature'; Magennis,
      'Images of Laughter'; Wilcox, *Humour in Anglo-Saxon Literature*; Bayless, 'Humour and the
      Comic'; Wilcox, 'Understatement and Incongruity'; and Wilcox, *Humour in Old English Literature*.
174 Arngart, 'The Durham Proverbs', p. 296 (no. 44). Angart interprets the first part of the proverb as
      'It is far from well' (p. 300), whereas Fred C. Robinson translates it as 'It is not well afar' ('Notes
      and Emendations', p. 364). My translation here is in accord with that of Marsden: 'Far and wide
      things aren't well', or in other words, 'Things are bad all over' (*The Cambridge Old English
      Reader*, p. 357).

Hunfridus Aurei Testiculi (Humphrey Gold-balls).[175] The unfortunate Godlef Crepunder Hwitel (Godlef Crawl-under-the-blanket) may have a nickname that reflected a childhood incident, or perhaps an even more embarrassing episode from adult life.[176] The sardonic nature of Anglo-Saxon wit is evident in the nickname of Rogerus Deus saluaet dominas (Roger 'God save the ladies').[177] It is not clear whether the so-called oxymoronic given names, such as Dægnieht (Day–night) or Wigfrith (War–peace), would also have been amusing to observers, if not to their owners.[178]

Whether Latin or vernacular, formal or casual, religious, secular, or profane, high-minded or down-to-earth, it is clear that Anglo-Saxon verbal art was relished by those who composed it, exchanged it, listened to it, and read it. Its communal nature meant that it was central to culture, and indeed its centrality ensured that it was communal. It was also entwined with most of the other modes of contemporary entertainment, most closely with music, but also essential to and celebrating (or occasionally condemning) the feasting, drinking, hunting, gaming, and merrymaking of its practitioners.

6 Festivals and Celebrations

The religious calendar established by the Anglo-Saxon Church suggests that the ecclesiastical establishment attempted to be the arbiter of how people spent their time, and in particular, when they fasted and abstained, when they (rarely) indulged, and when they were allowed to give way to joy, preferably pious joy. Evidence as to how devoutly these mandates were followed is not abundant, but the records do show that despite ecclesiastical disapproval, even church holidays often became occasions of enthusiastic secular merrymaking. A few types of non-religious celebration also make appearances in the record, and it is clear that many occasions known to be raucous celebrations later in history had started to gain that reputation even at this early date.

Fairs and markets are typically sites of carousing, bringing people together from across a wide span of geography and enriching some of them, a prime opportunity for celebration. It is more than likely, then, that such events provided occasion for merriment among the Anglo-Saxons. The Domesday Book lists sixty markets in England, though the fact that fourteen counties have no markets noted at all suggests that the actual number must have been greater. Many of these markets were tied to church festivals, not for reasons of piety but simply because church celebrations meant that people would be gathered from far and wide,

---

[175] Alfred appears in Biddle, *Winchester in the Early Middle Ages*, p. 50; Humphrey in Tengvik, *Old English Bynames*, p. 285.

[176] Clark, *Words, Names, and History*, p. 284.   [177] Tengvik, *Old English Bynames*, p. 389.

[178] Colman, *The Grammar of Names*, p. 42.

providing a prime opportunity for buying and selling.[179] Hence fairs tended to develop alongside religious feast days. These might occur once per year, such as the annual market at Stow in Lincolnshire,[180] or multiple times per year, associated with a sequence of various church festivals.

Commentators predictably deplored the practice of frivolities at such times; the *Canons of Edgar* warned against celebrating feast days 'hæðenra leoða and deofles gamena' ('of heathen songs and devil's games').[181] Contemporary records from the Continent show that religious festivals often served as an occasion for bawdy songs, round dances (particularly in the churchyard), and dressing up in animal costumes or the clothes of the opposite sex; official complaints about such fooleries were continual.[182]

Some religious festivals, such as Christmas, appear to have been accompanied by secular merriment across the country, but other festivals were undoubtedly celebrated only locally. Abundant evidence of such local festivals survives from later centuries, but the sources are not detailed enough to permit more than a glimpse of these from the Anglo-Saxon period. One modern survival that may suggest an Anglo-Saxon progenitor is the Abbots Bromley horn dance, still practised in the village of Abbots Bromley, Staffordshire. The dance does not appear in the written record until 1532, when it was recorded as being practised at Christmas, on New Year's, and on Twelfth Day (Epiphany), but other evidence suggests much earlier origins. If the reindeer antlers, radiocarbon-dated between 998 and 1269, were used for a dance at that date, as they are now, this may be a rare clue to the presence of secular ceremonial festivals as early as the tenth century.[183]

Weddings were presumably also celebratory. Brides wore festive clothes for the occasion, as is clear from the fact that Bede criticised the nuns of Coldingham for spending their leisure hours in 'texendis subtilioribus indumentis operam dant, quibus aut se ipsas ad uicem sponsarium ... adornent' ('weaving elaborate garments with which to adorn themselves as if they were brides').[184] The *Rule of Chrodegang* testified that dancing and the singing of love-songs and bawdy tunes were practised at weddings, and so warned clerics away from them.[185] The Old English version of the *Rule*, however, is

---

[179] On this and the development of markets, see Sawyer, 'Early Fairs and Markets' and Britnell, *The Commercialisation of English Society*.

[180] Sawyer, *Anglo-Saxon Charters*, no. 1478; Harmer, '*Chipping* and *Market*'.

[181] 'On Clofesho', in Haddan and Stubbs, *Councils and Ecclesiastical Documents*, vol. III, p. 368 (no. 16). On the *Canons of Edgar*: Wulfstan, *Wulfstan's Canons of Edgar*, pp. 6–7 (no. 18).

[182] For many details of these complaints, see Filotas, *Pagan Survivals*, pp. 154–82.

[183] Buckland, 'The Reindeer Antlers', pp. 1–8; the radiocarbon-dating results have been amended by calibration using IntCal13, the latest calibration available. On the horn dance, see Rice, *Abbots Bromley*, pp. 67–99 and Bayless, 'Fuller Brooch', pp. 206–07.

[184] Bede, *Bede's Ecclesiastical History*, ed. Colgrave and Mynors, pp. 424–27 (iv. 25).

[185] Napier, *The Old English Version*, pp. 78–79.

a translation of the eighth-century Latin original from Metz and so not a certain witness to the festivities at English weddings rather than Continental ones, although it is reasonable to assume that English weddings were similarly festive. Weddings as practised by resident Vikings certainly involved drinking, as is clear from the fact that the king Harthacnut died suddenly 'swa þæt he æt his drince stod' ('as he stood at his drink') at a wedding in Lambeth at 1042.[186]

The most local celebrations of all must have been birthday celebrations, although Ælfric reprimanded those who might be tempted to imitate Herod and throw a party: 'We ne moton ure gebyrdtide to nanum freolsdæge mid idelum mærsungum awendan ne ure acennednysse on swylcum gemynde habban, ac we sceolon urne endenextan dæg mid behreowsunge ⁊ dædbote forhradian'[187] ('We must not turn our birthday into a feasting-day with frivolous celebrations, nor keep the day of our being born with such commemorations, but we should anticipate our last day with repentance and penance').

Many other celebrations were tied to the cycles of the year, whether calendrical or seasonal. Some indication of the days felt to be important can be gleaned from the laws of King Alfred, which designated:

> Eallum frioum monnum ðas dagas sien forgifene, butan þeowum monnum ⁊ esnewyrhtan: xii dagas on gehhol ⁊ ðone dæg þe Crist ðone deofol oferswiðde ⁊ sanctus Gregorius gemynd-dæg ⁊ vii dagas to eastron ⁊ vii ofer ⁊ an dæg æt sancte Petres tide ⁊ sancte Paules ⁊ on hærfeste ða fullan wican ær sancta Marian mæssan ⁊ æt eallra haliga weorðunge anne dæg; ⁊ iiii Wodnesdagas on iiii ymbrenwicum ðeowum monnum eallum sien forgifen.[188]

> (To all free men let these days be given, except to slaves and *esnas*: twelve days at Yule, and the day that Christ overpowered the devil [15 February], and St Gregory's commemoration day [12 March], and seven days before Easter and seven after, and one day at St Peterstide and St Paul's [29 June], and at the harvest the full week before St Mary's mass [15 August], and one day at the honouring of All Saints [1 November], and let four Wednesdays on the four Ember weeks be given to all slaves.)

These days were designated holidays most likely in their identity as holy days, and intended to free workers to attend church; but people do tend to celebrate leisure time with activities other than prayer, and it is reasonable to suppose that some if not all of these occasions saw such celebration.

---

[186] Cubbin, *The Anglo-Saxon Chronicle, Vol. 6: MS. D*, s.v. 1042.

[187] Ælfric, *Ælfric's Catholic Homilies*, ed. Clemoes, p. 454 (no. XXXIII, lines 90–93).

[188] Jurasinski and Oliver, *The Laws of Alfred*, p. 348; this section, which Jurasinski and Oliver label 46, is 43 in other editions of Alfred's laws. Ember Days were four three-day periods of fasting and prayer, one in each season; they do not seem to have been associated with any particular merrymaking. The translation is my own.

The calendar year began with New Year's Day, although when that took place was variable: by some reckonings the year began at Christmas, by others in early January, or sometimes in March or September.[189] It is also not clear to what extent ordinary people regarded the various dates used by chroniclers, clerics, or distant government officials as definitive, and thereby celebrated the new year on those particular days. Ælfric noted that the first of January was often called 'geares dæge', 'Year's Day', which he specifies as the first day of the year, suggesting that that date was the one commonly regarded as beginning the new year.[190] Whichever day was identified, people regarded it as significant. Ælfric writes: 'Nu wigliað stunte men menigfealde wigelunda on þisum dæge mid micclum gedwylde æfter hæðenum gewunan ongean hyra cristendom, swilce hi magon heora lif gelengan oððe heora gesundfulnysse'[191] ('Now foolish men are accustomed to practice many kinds of divination on this day, with much unholiness, according to heathen customs, opposing their Christianity, so that they may lengthen their lives or their health').

A few prognostics associated with the New Year have survived.[192] One bases the fortune of the new year on the direction of the wind on New Year's Eve, another on the day of the week that New Year's Day falls upon. The practice of divination does not necessarily imply that New Year's was a time of merriment, although such rites are often practised in high spirits; but they do show that people regarded these days as distinct and special in ways not governed by the church, and such days are often distinguished by celebration.

Once the Twelve Days of Christmas were over, agricultural work might begin, and in later centuries the traditional day for such a beginning was known as Plough Monday, a time recognised with ceremony and merrymaking.[193] Such an occasion is reflected in the *Rectitudines*, which specifies that workers should have 'gytfeorm for yrðe', a 'drinking-feast for ploughing', suggesting that the occasion was similarly marked by celebration, and officially sponsored celebration at that.[194]

---

[189] Godden, 'New Year's Day'; Harrison, 'The Beginning of the Year'; for a summary of the dates and issues, see Parker, *Winters in the World*, pp. 77–80.

[190] Ælfric, *Ælfric's Catholic Homilies*, ed. Clemoes, p. 228.

[191] Ælfric, *Ælfric's Catholic Homilies*, ed. Clemoes, p. 229. In Ælfric, *Ælfric's Catholic Homilies*, ed. Godden, p. 46, the editor proposes that Ælfric has derived ideas of these practices from the written tradition of prognostics on the Continent, but New Year's prognostics are common enough across the world so there is no reason to think they were not practised in England as well.

[192] Liuzza, *Anglo-Saxon Prognostics*, pp. 491–95; Chardonnens, *Anglo-Saxon Prognostics*, pp. 491–500 (no. 17).

[193] Hutton, *The Stations of the Sun*, pp. 124–33; Roud, *The English Year*, pp. 19–25.

[194] *Rectitudines singularum personarum* 21.4, in Liebermann, *Die Gesetze der Angelsachsen*, vol. I, p. 452.

As the year progressed, the self-denying season of Lent approached. The first day of Lent is Ash Wednesday, and the three days preceding Ash Wednesday are now known as Shrovetide, a period that offers the last opportunities for self-indulgence before the austerity of Lent. In later centuries this became a notable period of licence and carnival.[195] Only the faintest indication of such licence can be glimpsed among the Anglo-Saxons. The week before Ash Wednesday was known as *cyswuce*, 'cheese-week', the final week in which cheese was permitted before the coming of Lent.[196] Whether this last week was the occasion for further indulgence is not attested, but the fact that the week was named after cheese, rather than after a religious element, suggests that food was the subject of greater attention than was piety.

Easter does not seem to have given rise to much frivolity – at least preachers and homilists do not complain about it – but the powerful did apparently hold feasts on the occasion, as when King Oswald and Bishop Aidan were petitioned by beggars at an Easter feast and ended up giving the petitioners the meal and the silver plate upon which it had been served.[197] Celebrations also took place lower on the social scale: workers were owed 'Easterfeorm', 'Easter fare', as specified in the *Rectitudines*.[198]

One of the biggest festivals of the year was Rogationtide, or the Days of Rogation, which formed the three days before Ascension Day, the sixth Thursday after Easter.[199] Called the *Gangdagas*, 'Walking Days', or the *Gebeddagas*, 'Prayer Days', the three-day period was marked by preaching, prayers, and procession around the countryside. By the time details of the festival are available, in the late twelfth century, the processors carried torches and banners signifying biblical personages, beginning with the dragon symbolising Pontius Pilate, followed by a lion symbolising Christ, followed by images of the saints.[200] These banners are not attested from the Anglo-Saxon period, but it is clear that the processions were substantial. The *Old English Martyrology* specified that a procession should be held from the third hour of the day to the ninth hour, and a homily by Ælfric specifies that they should carry 'þa halige godspell and oðre halignessa, mid þam we sceolon bletsian ure þa eorðlican speda, þæt synd æceras and wudu and ure ceap'[201] ('the holy gospel and other holy things, with which we should bless our earthly prosperity, which are fields

[195] Hutton, *Stations of the Sun*, pp. 151–68; Roud, *English Year*, pp. 60–87.
[196] Tupper, 'Anglo-Saxon Dæg-Mæl', pp. 191, 199, 216–17.
[197] Bede, *Bede's Ecclesiastical History*, ed. Colgrave and Mynors, pp. 230–31 (iii. 6).
[198] *Rectitudines* 21.4, in Liebermann, *Die Gesetze der Angelsachsen*, vol. I, p. 452.
[199] On Rogationtide, particularly its theological aspects, see Kramer, *Between Heaven and Earth*, pp. 147–200.
[200] Hutton, *Stations of the Sun*, pp. 277–87.
[201] Bazire and Cross, *Eleven Old English Rogationtide Homilies*, p. 112 (Homily 8, lines 111–13).

and woods and our cattle'). One of the *Vercelli Homilies* elaborates on this, specifying again that they must carry the Gospel and holy relics of the saints, which (the homily explains) are constituted of their hair or parts of their body or clothes.[202] These processions were attended by throngs of people, so many that the account of the vision seen by Leofric, earl of Mercia, used the image to paint a picture of a crowd: 'Þa geseah he swyþe mycele weorud swylce on gangdagan'[203] ('Then he saw a very great crowd, such as on the Walking Days'). There are some suggestions that the procession involved a number of 'stations' at which it would stop and a sermon would be preached. The procession around the lands evolved, in later periods, into more explicit boundary rituals, eventually becoming the practice of 'beating the bounds', though this had diverged from its associations with Rogation and prayer.[204]

As early as the eighth century the religious aspects of Rogationtide were accompanied by secular festivities: the Council of Clofesho in 747 fulminated against the 'ludis et equorum cursibus, et epulis majoribus', 'games and horse races, and great feasts', practised on the Days of Rogation.[205] One of the *Vercelli Homilies* warned against 'idele spæca & tæflunga & gebeorscipas', 'frivolous speech and gaming and drinking-feasts', which were forbidden at all times, but especially on the Days of Rogation.[206] It is unclear whether these were specially practised at Rogationtide or whether this merely forms a warning against frivolity, but the edict from Clofesho suggests that these mean that Rogationtide came to be an occasion for amusements as well as for piety.

Midsummer (*midsumor* or *midsumer*) and midsummer eve (*midsumeres mæsseæfen*) were also popular holidays, forming a counterpart to Christmas, which was known as *midwinter*. Like Christmas, midsummer was regarded as a powerful day to practise certain kinds of magic.[207] It also appears to have been a time for games and sports, at least among young people: an eleventh-century story from Wilton Abbey tells of a teenage boy who meant to keep vigil at a shrine on St John's Eve, but was distracted by the traditional games: 'nocturnis puerorum ludis, qui in eadem festiuitate iuxta ritum antiquorum sollemniter celebrantur, quadam animi leuitate uacare cepit'[208] ('he started to abandon [the vigil], engaging with a certain lightness of mind in the nighttime games of the boys, which are

---

[202] Scragg, *The Vercelli Homilies*, pp. 228–29 (no. xii, lines 14–34).

[203] Stokes, 'The Vision of Leofric', p. 548; my translation.

[204] Roud, *English Year*, pp. 243–47.

[205] Haddan and Stubbs, *Councils and Ecclesiastical Documents*, vol. III, p. 368 (no. 16).

[206] Homily for Monday in Rogationtide (no. XIX), in Scragg, *Vercelli Homilies*, p. 320, lines 90–91.

[207] Van Arsdall, *Medieval Herbal Remedies*, pp. 146, 210. On these festivities, see also Section 1. The limitations of claims about midsummer festivities at this date are outlined in Billington, 'The Midsummer Solstice'.

[208] Wilmart, 'La légende', p. 301.

celebrated with due ceremony at that festival according to ancient practice'). It is a shame that no details of these games survive.

Lammas (*hlafmæsse*, 'bread mass', also known as *hlafsenunga*, 'bread blessing'), on 1 August, was similarly regarded as a powerful and potentially festive day. It signalled the beginning of the harvest, with the bread traditionally blessed on that day being the first made from the harvest.[209] The day was also thought to be powerful for working crop magic, and the blessed bread was thought to have special protective powers.[210] Harvest was traditionally a time of ceremony and rejoicing, with abundant evidence from later centuries. In particular the harvest was often marked with ceremonies surrounding the last sheaf, the celebration of which was often attended by feasting and carousing.[211] The *Rectitudines* give some hint of these, specifying three harvest-time occasions at which festivities would be held: 'bendfeorm for ripe ... hreacmete ... æt cornlade hreaccopp'[212] ('a binding-feast for harvest ... a rick-meal ... at corn-carrying, a rick-cup').

The final large-scale preparations for winter were probably made on St Martin's Day, or Martinmas (*Martines mæsse*), on 11 November, typically a time of revelry and feasting accompanying the slaughter of livestock that could not be over-wintered. Bede recounted that the pagan Anglo-Saxons had called November *Blotmonath*, 'the month of sacrifices', or alternately *Blodmonath*, 'the month of blood [viz. sacrifices]', because the pagans made sacrifices to their gods in that month.[213] That the Anglo-Saxons celebrated the day, or the season, with feasting and revelry can only be conjectured, as no specific evidence survives; but in later centuries Martinmas was associated with so much carousing that St Martin was informally transformed into a saint of mischief and foolery.[214] It was also a time of ball games, played with the inflated bladders of the slaughtered pigs, and it is reasonable to assume this was true in Anglo-Saxon England as in later centuries.

There survive only the barest hints that Christmas was a time of festivity, but if saints' days were celebrated with feasting, Christmas was likely a time for even greater celebration. The holiday was known in Old English as *midwinter*, *Cristesmæsse*, or *Geola* (Yule); it lasted twelve days and, as mentioned, King Alfred's laws specified that freemen should receive all twelve as holiday, the longest period of festivity specified in the law

---

[209] Lammas is noted as the day of bread blessing in Rauer, *The Old English Martyrology*, pp. 150–51; for *hlafsenunga*, see p. 150.

[210] Jolly, 'Prayers from the Field', pp. 109–11.

[211] Frazer, *Spirits of the Corn*, vol. I, ch. V (titled 'The Corn-Mother and the Corn-Maiden in Northern Europe', vol. 7 of *The Golden Bough*). Frazier's interpretations are no longer regarded as reliable, but his compendious examples of corn-mother and corn-maiden traditions amply demonstrate how widespread and popular the tradition was.

[212] *Rectitudines* 21.4, in Liebermann, *Die Gesetze der Angelsachsen*, vol. I, pp. 452–53.

[213] Bede, *De temporum ratione liber*, p. 332 (cap. XV.49).

[214] For later tradition in England, see Walsh, 'Medieval English Martinmesse'.

codes.[215] The *Rectitudines* specified that workers should be granted a *winterfeorm*, or in the Latin version, 'firma natalis Domini', 'fare of the birth of the Lord', with the implication that the fare would form a feast.[216] The holiday was accordingly a time of indulgent feasting, which led Ælfric to warn against 'oferfylle and oferdrence', 'too much eating and too much drinking', at Christmas.[217] It formed a time of abundance in multiple ways: the *Rectitudines* enjoined that shepherds should receive twelve nights' worth of dung at midwinter: what may to modern ears sound like a disagreeable present was a valuable fertiliser for kitchen gardens, or it might be used as fuel for hearths.[218] Christmas Day was also thought to be a time of magical power, so that prognostics were created that predicted fortunes depending on whether the sun shone on the Twelve Days, the direction of the wind, or the day of the week on which Christmas fell.[219] Thus the old year drew to a close and the new year entered, with its own round of festivals and merrymaking, both denounced and celebrated.

7 Hunting and Sport

Diuinis enim expeditus officiis quibus libenter cotidiana intendebat deuotione, iocundabatur plurimum coram se allatis accipitribus uel huius generis auibus, uel certe delectabatur applausibus multorum motuum canibus. His et talibus interdum deducebat diem, et in his tantummodo ex natura uidebatur aliquam mundi captare delectationem.

(After divine service, which he gladly and devoutly attended every day, he took much pleasure in hawks and birds of that kind which were brought before him, and was really delighted by the baying and scrambling of the hounds. In these and such like activities he sometimes spent the day, and it was in these alone that he seemed naturally inclined to snatch some worldly pleasure.)[220]

— *The Life of King Edward*

[215] Jurasinski and Oliver, *Laws of Alfred*, p. 348 (section 46, or 43 in other editions).

[216] *Rectitudines/Quadripartitus* 21.4, in Liebermann, *Die Gesetze der Angelsachsen*, vol. I, p. 452.

[217] Ælfric, *Ælfric's Catholic Homilies: The Second Series,* ed. Godden, p. 11 (Sermon I, 'De Natale Domini').

[218] *Rectitudines* 12, in Liebermann, *Die Gesetze der Angelsachsen*, vol. I, p. 451.

[219] Chardonnens, *Anglo-Saxon Prognostics*, pp. 483–85, 491–500; Liuzza, *Anglo-Saxon Prognostics*, pp. 483–85, 489–90, 496–97; Cesario, 'The Shining of the Sun'.

[220] Barlow, *The Life of King Edward*, pp. 40–41 (cap. vi).

Edward the Confessor was celebrated both for his religious devotion and for his delight in hawking and hunting, as evidenced by the passage from his biography cited as the epigraph to this section. In his love of the hunt he was not alone: over the course of the Anglo-Saxon period hunting and hawking were increasingly enjoyed by the elite, so much so that supporting elite men's leisure came to be a source of employment for men of lower status. The results of such hunts – feasts and the ritual distribution of the meat – demarcated status and served a community function as well, as we shall see.

Other sport, some more widespread across the social spectrum, included ball games, horse racing, foot racing, wrestling, swimming, ice skating, and animal baiting. This roster of early sport leaves out many that we might expect, sport that is known either from Scandinavian examples or from later medieval English sources. These pursuits, absent from Anglo-Saxon records but likely to have been practised, include wrestling, cockfighting, dogfighting, and even possibly, as in Iceland, horsefighting, a brutal spectacle brought about by inducing two stallions to fight over a mare.[221]

The other element missing from records of early sport is gender: although later English accounts suggest that women sometimes participated in some sporting pursuits, in the Anglo-Saxon period women do not show up in the record of such recreation. The records therefore show principally the sporting enjoyments of elite men.

For all levels of society, hunting might serve as a means of putting meat on the table, but it was only the elite who had the leisure to practise the hunt in ceremonial fashion. For those high on the social ladder, hunting was a great deal more than sustenance: as one historian has observed, in agricultural societies such as Anglo-Saxon England, 'hunting is generally a highly ritualized social action, bound up with power, landownership and the communication of identity'.[222] Hunting may even have helped shape the landscape, if, as has been proposed, hunting parks or enclosures were introduced in the late Anglo-Saxon period.[223]

The evidence suggests that before the mid seventh century, hunting was not a regular source of food, but as such was practised principally in times of dearth. Evidence for this comes from animal bones: from this early period such bones were usually not food waste; instead, animal parts survive principally as ritual objects, perhaps used as amulets, in grave goods.[224] This suggests a ritual,

---

[221] For a comprehensive look at later medieval English pastimes, see Reeves, *Pleasures and Pastimes*; for Scandinavian examples, including horsefighting, see Gogosz, 'Hver er sterkastr?' and Martin, 'Sports and Games'.

[222] Sykes, 'Deer', p. 175.

[223] Sykes, 'Deer', p. 175; Hooke, *The Landscape*; Lilliard, 'The Deer Parks'; and Sykes, 'Woods and the Wild', p. 339.

[224] Sykes, 'Deer', p. 178.

magico-mystical aspect to the hunt, and would provide at least a partial motivation for hunting that fits neither into the strictly utilitarian nor into the recreational category.

By the late Anglo-Saxon period, however, hunting seems to have been regarded primarily as a recreational marker of status. Asser's *Life of King Alfred*, for example, emphasises Alfred's hunting prowess, classing it among the gifts bestowed by God: 'In omni venatoria arte industrius venator incessabiliter laborat non in vanum; nam incomparabilis omnibus peritia et felicitate in illa arte, sicut et in ceteris omnibus Dei donis, fuit' ('An enthusiastic huntsman, he strives continually in every branch of hunting, and not in vain; for no one else could approach him in skill and success in that activity, just as in all other gifts of God').[225]

Asser champions Alfred's noblility by describing his determination to perform the duties of his station despite Viking invasions, bodily afflictions, and other disruptions. Hunting and maintaining the requisites for the hunt were a conspicuous part of those noble pursuits: 'Interea tamen rex, inter bella et praesentis vitae frequentia impedimenta, necnon paganorum infestationes et cotidianas corporis infirmitates, et regni gubernacula regere, et omnem venandi artem agere, aurifices et artifices suos omnes et falconarios et accipitrarios canicularios quoque docere' ('Meanwhile the king, amidst the wars and numerous interruptions of this present life – not to mention the Viking attacks and his continual bodily infirmities – did not refrain from directing the government of the kingdom, pursing all manner of hunting; giving instruction to all his goldsmiths and craftsmen as well as to his falconers, hawk-trainers and dog-keepers').[226]

Elswhere Asser reiterates that hunting is a high-status endeavour, referring to 'venatoriae ... et ceteris artibus, quae nobilibus conveniunt' ('hunting ... and other skills appropriate to noblemen').[227] Deer and boar seem to have been the most common objects of pursuit; the fact that both were edible meant that a ritual presentation of the choicest parts could be enjoyed at the subsequent feast. In the late Anglo-Saxon period the practices denoting status seem to have changed, with evidence from elite sites showing that all parts of the deer were consumed rather than distributed. This may demonstrate that the elite were 'privatizing venison and consuming it as a marker of social difference'.[228]

---

[225] Asser, *Asser's Life of King Alfred*, p. 20 (ch. 22); translation by Keynes and Lapidge, *Alfred the Great*, p. 75.

[226] Asser, *Asser's Life of King Alfred*, p. 59 (ch. 76); translation by Keynesand Lapidge, *Alfred the Great*, p. 91.

[227] Asser, *Asser's Life of King Alfred*, p. 58 (ch. 75); translation by Keynes and Lapidge, *Alfred the Great*, p. 90.

[228] Sykes, 'Woods', p. 339.

A stag hunt depicted in the tenth-century *Vita S. Dunstani* suggests that the whole apparatus of high-status hunts known from later periods was already in force, with the hunters pursuing the quarry on horseback, aided by hounds and the blowing of horns.[229] The consolidation of such hunting as a high-status sport was furthered with the arrival of William the Conqueror. The Anglo-Saxon Chronicle for 1087 reported that the Conqueror reserved the hunt for himself to such an extent that he decreed that others who encroached on his deer should be blinded, and that he established enclosures for hunting.

However recreational the hunt in intention, the fact that it involved weapons and wilderness made the enterprise dangerous. It is no accident that so many later medieval romances depicted hunting as a jumping-off point to adventure and misadventure. Thus another theme runs through accounts of hunting: hunting that leads to the death of the huntsman. Examples are numerous: some were genuine accidents, some murders disguised as accidents, and some merely wild rumours, but all participated in the same theme – the hunt as a site of mortal danger. The boy king St Kenelm was lured into the woods on the pretext of a hunt, and then murdered; Asser described the death of the Frankish king Carloman, killed by a boar in a boar hunt; King Edgar was said to have been in love with a woman who had married the duplicitous ealdorman Æthelwald, whereupon Edgar invited Æthelwald out hunting and murdered him; Edward the Martyr was said to have been hunting when he was murdered at Corfe Castle; Ealdorman Ælfhelm was rumoured to have been lured out hunting and then killed under the orders of Eadric Streona; Richard, the son of William the Conqueror, was killed by an overhanging hazel branch while on a hunt; and Richard's brother, the king, William Rufus, was killed by the arrow of a fellow huntsman while out hunting. Even the account of hunting in the *Vita S. Dunstani* involves accidental death, when the stag along with the pursuing hounds plunge to their deaths in Cheddar Gorge. The perilous aspects of the hunt lent it a daredevil type of reputation, akin to the dangerous sports of the modern rich such as heli skiing or attempting to summit Everest.

Closely allied to sport hunting were the practices of hawking and falconry. The two practices occupy a similar niche in aristocratic culture, the key difference being the method of hunting: falcons hunt by striking from a great height, and so need open countryside, while hawks pursue their quarry at low altitude and thus can hunt in wooded or brushy country.[230] Among the most common quarries were cranes, herons, and ducks, each a part of the diet of the Anglo-

---

[229] Winterbottom and Lapidge, *Early Lives*, p. 48 (ch. 14.1–2); Flight, 'Aristocratic Deer Hunting'.

[230] On medieval English practices generally, see Oggins, *The Kings and Their Hawks*, pp. 10–35. Further details are provided by Wallis, '"As the Falcon Her Bells"' and Dobney and Jaques, 'Avian Signatures'.

Saxons, so that the kills likely formed a ritual part of feasting, on par with offerings of venison and boar. It also formed a seasonal sport, being practised in the autumn and winter. Two eleventh-century English calendars depict hawking as a characteristic of October: BL Cotton Julius A.VI, fol. 7v depicts a standing man with a hawk, and BL Cotton Tiberius B.V/1, fol. 7v is a sumptuous depiction of a man on foot and another on horseback, both holding hawks, in a wilderness scene populated by the ducks and crane they intend to pursue.

Hawking to provide food for the table might be practised by a person of any status who had the time and opportunity to train a hawk, but like aristocratic hunting, as a pastime it was the province of the mighty. The mighty also often included the high-status members of the clergy, whose attachment to falconry appears in the earliest records. Around 745, Boniface, heading an Anglo-Saxon mission on the Continent, sent a hawk and two falcons to King Ethelbald of Mercia.[231] Boniface was evidently known for his liking for falconry, or at least for obtaining birds, as a few years later King Ethelbert of Kent wrote a letter asking Boniface for two falcons who could bring down cranes, complaining that compliant birds were hard to obtain in Kent.[232] A number of disapproving reformers admonished the clergy for their love of such pastimes. Eadmer complained that before they had mended their ways in response to a miracle, the monks of Christ Church, Canterbury had paraded around with horses, hounds, and hawks and 'more comitum potius quam monachorum uitam age-bant' ('led the life of counts more than of monks'),[233] adding another confirm-ation to the idea that such activities were associated with the nobility.

That formal hunting should be the province of the aristocracy makes sense, as it took considerable resources to provide the horses, hounds, dog-keepers, and other accoutrements. Supplying these became an obligation of those lower on the social scale. The Domesday Book records that Wiltshire, Oxfordshire, Warwickshire, Leicester, and Worcester had the obligation to provide £10 annually for a hawk for the king, or in some cases they could provide the hawk directly. Northamptonshire had an obligation of £10 for a hawk, £42 for dogs, and £20 for a huntsman's horse.[234] Berkshire men were required to drive game, and those who failed to show up were fined fifty shillings.[235] A number of records also granted certain institutions such as churches and monasteries exemptions from the obligation to put up the king's hawks, hounds, horses, or huntsmen; sometimes these exemptions were purchased, showing what

---

[231] Oggins, *The Kings*, p. 38, citing 'S. Bonifatii et Lulli epistolae', vol. I, p. 337.

[232] Oggins, *The Kings*, p. 38, citing 'S. Bonifatii et Lulli epistolae'', vol. I, p. 392.

[233] *Miraculi S. Dunstani*, in Eadmer, *Eadmer of Canterbury*, p. 189 (ch. 19); my translation.

[234] Domesday Book I, fols. 64b, 154b, 219, 238, 230, 172.

[235] Williams and Martin, *Domesday Book*, p. 137.

a burden the obligations had become.[236] The recreations of the mighty were not merely more elaborate than those of the lowly, they were literally at the expense of the lowly.

Another recreation which must have been practised by those higher on the social ladder was sport involving horses, for which one presumably needed to be able to afford a horse. Aldhelm warns his correspondent Æthilwald against indulging 'in equitandi uagatione culpabili' ('blameworthy wanderings on horseback').[237] Horse racing also appears in several texts, often as a spontaneous expression of high spirits. Bede told the story of a cleric named Heribald, who as a young man had succumbed to the temptation to join the local youths in racing their horses against each other, and met with an accident.[238] The horse races in *Beowulf* (lines 864–67 and 916–17) were also spontaneous, forming part of the general rejoicing after the defeat of Grendel. On the matter of horse racing the church again stepped in to admonish those who might try to mix piety and sport: in 747 the Council of *Clofesho* warned against frivolities like horse racing on the Days of Rogation, which should not be 'admixtis vanitatibus, uti mos est plurimis ... id est, in ludis et equorum cursibus, et epulis majoribus' ('mixed with vanities, as is the custom of many ... that is, in games and horse-races, and great feasts').[239] In the post-Conquest period, William of Malmesbury reported that Hugh the Great of France tried to woo the daughter of Athelstan by sending her spices, gems, and 'equos cursores plurimos cum faleris' ('many racehorses with trappings').[240] If this is not an anachronistic imputation of later culture to the pre-Conquest period, it would mean that by the tenth century the sport had evolved sufficiently enough for the king to keep horses specifically for racing purposes.

Mentions of foot races are even rarer, but one survives in the *Vita* of Bishop Wulfstan of Winchester (*c.* 1008–1095), transmitted by William of Malmesbury, and quoted in Section 2. Like horse racing, the race appears to have been informal and spontaneous. Unusually, the saint (in this case Wulfstan) is depicted as excelling in the sport rather than reprimanding the participants; in this instance he wins the race.

Ball games were very popular in later medieval England, and took numerous forms: some with bats, some with sticks resembling hockey sticks, some

[236] Oggins, *The Kings*, p. 39.

[237] William of Malmesbury, *Gesta Pontificum Anglorum* ed. and trans. Winterbottom and Thomson, vol. I, pp. 512–13 (Book V, cap. 193.2).

[238] *Historia ecclesiastica* V.6; Bede, *Ecclesiastical History of the English People*, trans. Sherley-Price, p. 273.

[239] Haddan and Stubbs, *Councils and Ecclesiastical Documents*, vol. III, p. 368 (no. 16).

[240] William of Malmesbury, *Gesta Regum Anglorum*, vol. I, p. 218 (cap. 135). My translation; the edition has 'swift horses' rather than 'racehorses'.

involving throwing the ball and others rolling it, and all manner of variations. Medieval Scandinavia shows a similar diversity of ball games. It is likely that Anglo-Saxon England had a variety as well, but records are scant. Races and ball games were probably behind place names such as Ganfield or Gamfield ('Game field') Hundred in Berkshire.[241] Bede mentions a ball game in describing the spherical shape of the globe, noting that the size of mountains and valleys does not alter its spherical nature: 'quamuis enormem montium ualliumque distantiam quantum in pila ludicra unum digitum tantum addere uel demere crediderim' ('I should think that even the enormous height of mountains and valleys is such that it would add or subtract only as much as a finger would add or subtract to a playing-ball').[242] A ball-and-stick game is mentioned as a sport of boys in the *Colloquy* of Ælfric Bata, but ball games were not restricted to children. William of Malmesbury recounts the legend of a man named Edmund who became a bishop after he had proposed it purely as a joke. William uses a euphonious Latin expression for the man's preference for games: 'mallet lusum pilae quam usum cucullae' ('he preferred a game of ball to the cowl').[243] In later medieval England, teams for ball games often included both men and women, but the participation of women in the early period is unclear.

Swimming as recreation, as well as life skill, must have been practised, though most historical records merely record drownings, particularly in settings of war.[244] The only evidence for swimming in fiction comes in *Beowulf*, where Beowulf and Breca have a swimming race (lines 506–17), or possibly, it has been argued, a rowing race, such as is known from Scandinavian texts.[245] Skill in swimming, among other talents, is also mentioned in *The Gifts of Men*, and it has been suggested that these have a parallel in lists of *íþróttir* or 'high-status masculine accomplishments' in Scandinavian texts such as *Rígsþula*, which classifies swimming as a characteristic of earls rather than of lowlier men.[246]

The practice of ice skating is attested by archaeological finds of cattle and horse bones shaped into skates. These survive from around the seventh century onwards; by the tenth century horse bones were favoured, suggesting that skates were made principally by those wealthy enough to own horses.[247] Skating had

---

[241] Crawford, *Childhood*, p. 139, citing Gelling, 'Some Meanings of "Stow"'.

[242] Bede, *De temporum ratione liber*, p. 380 (cap. 32.8–10).

[243] William of Malmesbury, *Gesta Pontificum*, vol. I, p. 410 (Book III, cap. 130.6–7); my translation.

[244] Trafford, 'Swimming in Anglo-Saxon England'.   [245] Earl, 'Beowulf's Rowing-Match'.

[246] Russom, 'A Germanic Concept of Nobility'; Trafford, 'Swimming', pp. 100–01. Swimming also forms part of a roster of manly skills belonging to the hero Cuchulainn in the *Táin Bó Cúalnge*, along with horsemanship, skill at board games, martial prowess, and other accomplishments; O'Rahilly, *Táin Bó Cúalnge*, p. 152.

[247] Riddler and Trzaska-Nartowsk, 'Chanting upon A Dunghill', pp. 119, 131; MacGregor, Mainman, and Rogers, *Craft, Industry, and Everyday Life*, p. 2005.

a utilitarian value, of course, allowing easy movement on rivers and water in frozen conditions, but those who have skates seem to take the opportunity to enjoy them, as evidenced by Bruegel's much later painting *Winter Landscape with Ice Skaters and Bird Trap*, showing skaters taking advantage of the ice just as the Anglo-Saxons must have done.

An intriguing early round-up of a number of sports is provided in Aldhelm's prose *De virginitate*, in which he constructs an elaborate metaphor of religious learning by comparing it to the training of Olympic athletes.[248] It is clear that the image of the Olympic athletes is derived from Classical sources, with the explicit addition of 1 Corinthians 9:24 ('all runneth indeed, but one receiveth the prize'), but presumably the varieties of sport made sense to Aldhelm, and so it may be cautiously proposed that similar sport may have been known in his time. The passage describes athletes wrestling, competing at spear throwing and archery, and in foot races, horse races, and rowing races. All these sports might have had practical uses in Anglo-Saxon England – unlike, for instance, Classical sports such as discus throwing – and so it would be unsurprising if these were contemporary practices.

Competition in any of these might have formed a spectator sport. More gruesome spectator sports involved inducing animals to fight, including boars and bears and almost certainly cocks, though these last are less surely attested at this period. Ælfric told the cautionary tale of a man who drank unwisely in Lent without a blessing on his cup, and immediately afterwards was killed by a boar from a boar-baiting.[249] Bear-baiting is also attested: it forms part of an illuminated initial in British Library Arundel 91, fol. 47v (from the second half of the eleventh century), and of the Bayeux Tapestry, where a man with a sword and a shield is pitted against a muzzled bear. It is unclear whether such bears were captured in Britain or whether they were imported. It was formerly thought that bears died out in England prior to the Anglo-Saxon period, but this idea was overturned by the discovery of a bear vertebra, radiocarbon-dated to between the early fifth and early sixth centuries, in a cave in North Yorkshire.[250] Bear claws and other parts appear in early Anglo-Saxon burials, apparently used as amulets; this suggests that bears were native at the time, though it is possible that the parts could have been imported as part of bearskins. A bear is depicted in the poem *Maxims II*, in conjunction with references to a hawk and a boar: 'Bera sceal on hæðe / eald and egesfull' ('The bear shall dwell on the heath, old and terrible') (lines 29–30). However, the

[248] Aldhelm, *Prosa de virginitate*, ed. Gwara, p. 230 (cap. 2); *Aldhelm: The Prose Works*, trans. Lapidge and Herren, p. 60 (cap. 2).

[249] Ælfric, *Lives of Saints*, p. 266 (no. 12, Ash Wednesday).

[250] Hammon, 'The Brown Bear', p. 100; see also O'Regan, 'The Presence of the Brown Bear'.

reference also comes soon after the description of a dragon, so the poem cannot serve as indisputable evidence of the presence of all its beasts in real life. The Domesday Book notes that Norwich was required to give the crown one bear and six dogs (presumably to bait the bear) annually, but whether these bears were native or had to be imported is open to question.[251]

The meaning and nuance of many of these practices is obscured by the limited nature of the evidence, but despite this it is clear that the Anglo-Saxons enjoyed a variety of sports. Some, like hunting and hawking, were enjoyed more by those who had the wealth and power to practise them than by those who were employed or compelled to support them; others such as ball games and spectator sports were open to wider levels of society, and can be glimpsed only dimly through the mists of history.

8 Games and Play

Hy twegen sceolon tæfle ymbsittan,   þenden him hyra torn toglide,
            . . . habban him gomen on borde.[252]

(Two shall sit together at the board game until their misery glides from them . . . they shall have joy/a game at the board.)
— *Maxims I*

Games in early medieval England were in many ways like food and drink: so commonplace that few bothered to describe them. Despite this, games, especially board games, carried great meaning for the Anglo-Saxons, to the extent that they typically form part of the grave goods of the powerful. They served as a bridge between the martial, serious aspects of life and the relaxed, playful parts, both the care of kings and the mighty. As in many cultures, board games had a religious dimension in some contexts; during the pagan period they were celebrated as an order-bestowing element of the creation of the world; in later sources they are cast in Christian allegorical terms.

In the modern English-speaking world, board games are considered trivial pastimes, or, as in examples such as chess, admittedly intellectual yet marginal to 'serious' culture. But even in the twenty-first-century world this view of board games is not universal. In the Asian world, for instance, the game of Go or Weiqi has a weighty central role in culture, as does Mancala/Oware in many African cultures. It is this kind of weight that board games held in Anglo-Saxon England and in surrounding contemporary cultures.

---

[251] Domesday Book fol. 116.

[252] Muir, *The Exeter Anthology*, vol. I, p. .256 (*Maxims* I(C), lines 181–82/43–44). For discussion of the grammatical problems in this and the succeeding line, see vol. II, p. 538.

Traditionally, most societies have assigned different kinds of games to different roles in culture. The classic formulation, in the words of foundational games anthropologists, is that 'Games of strategy are related to social systems, games of chance are related to religious beliefs.'[253] This does not mean that even games of strategy are wholly separate from religious beliefs. Complex games of skill are regarded as tests of power and prowess; such games are often considered the special province of elite leaders, and sometimes the game is restricted to certain groups, although often games associated with the elite are nevertheless widespread throughout society. Moreover, such games are often associated with the power of the gods, with the ultimate player of the game envisioned as the chief god, who orders the game much as he arranges society. By contrast, games of chance are often envisioned as tests of the relationship between the player and the supernatural powers who control the roll of the die or the disposition of chance. Although Christianity has somewhat tempered these associations in the instance of early medieval England, components of these remained present.

We can see evidence of the central role of board games in early English culture in several of the poems enumerating the variety of people and activities in the culture. *The Gifts of Men*, for instance, outlines the talents of various kinds of men, including weapon-makers, the pious, the good thane in the mead hall, and those skilled with horses. The poem continues:

> Sum domas con,   þær dryhtguman
> ræd eahtiað.   Sum bið hrædtæfle.
> Sum bið gewittig   æt winþege,
> beorhyrde god.   Sum bið bylda til
> ham to hebbanne . . . .[254]

> ('One is skilled at judgements, when men
> deliberate counsel. One is quick at the board game.
> One is expert at the wine-taking,
> a good barkeeper. One is a good builder
> to raise a house . . . .')

Similarly, *The Fortunes of Men* lays out the variety of skills and fates in the world, all bestowed by God, who gives

> sumum eadwelan,   sumum earfeþa dæl,
> sumum geogoþe glæd,   sumum guþe blæd,
> gewealdenne wigplegan,   sumum wyrp oþþe scyte,

---

[253] Roberts, Arth, and Bush, 'Games in Culture', p. 604.
[254] *The Gifts of Men* (lines 72–76), in Muir, *The Exeter Anthology*, vol. I, p. 139.

torhtlicne tiir,   sumum tæfle cræft,
bleobordes gebregd. Sume boceras
weorþað wisfæste .... [255]

('to some riches; to some a portion of trouble;
to some, bright youth; to some glory in battle,
to rule in battle-play; to some a throw or a shot,
shining glory; to some skill at the board game,
moves on the coloured board. Some become
wise scholars ....')

In both poems the game forms a bridge between activities. In *The Gifts of Men*, it makes its appearance between the judgements levied in the hall and the time of feasting, as indeed it is appropriate to both wise judgement and to feasting and merrymaking. In *The Fortunes of Men*, the game appears between the vigour of battle and the quieter skills of the scholar, as it is a martial activity practised in the quiet of reflection. The board game was in effect a liminal space, partaking of multiple aspects of life: the seriousness of conflict and battle, the intellectual skills wielded in wise judgement, and the pleasures of the peaceable hall. For these reasons skill at the board game became an emblem of sagacity and power.

The elite status and associations of the board game were apparent not only in early England, but widely in the cultures of early medieval north-west Europe. In the Old Norse *Orkneyinga Saga*, for example, Kali Kolsson, later earl of Orkney, lists his skill at the board game *tafl* first among his qualifications to be a leader.[256] In Ireland, laws specified that the education of the son of a king or noble should include skill at the board games *fidchell* and *brannuigecht*, and numerous tales depict kings playing the board game as a ritual daily practice.[257] In medieval Wales, the offices of chancellor, judge of the court, and head of the royal retinue all involved a ritual bestowing of a *tawlbwrdd* (*tæfl*) set by the king, sometimes with the stipulation that the recipient could never pass it on to others either by sale or by gift.[258]

The high status of board games may be clear, but identifying the games requires detective work; this is somewhat simpler for the games of other parts of northern Europe, particularly for Scandinavia, where numerous game boards and descriptions of games survive, and for Ireland and Wales. But in England, climactic conditions meant that, although gaming pieces survive in quantity, the game boards themselves, made of wood, have perished, and this hinders an understanding of which games were played. So although there is abundant evidence that board

---

[255] *The Fortunes of Men* (ll, lines 67–72), in Muir, *The Exeter Anthology*, vol. I, pp. 155–56.

[256] Guðmundsson, *Orkneyinga saga*, p. 130 (cap. 58); the English translation is Pálsson and Edwards, *Orkneyinga Saga*, p. 108 (ch. 58).

[257] Kelly, *Early Irish Farming*, p. 452; Binchy, *Corpus iuris Hibernici*, vol. V, p. 1760, ll. 33–34.

[258] Lewis, 'Gwerin Ffristial a Thawlbwrdd', p. 191.

games were played and valued, the details of those games are patchy and not easily interpreted. Vocabulary confuses more than it clarifies the matter. From glossaries and a few mentions in literary works, it is clear that the Old English term used to denote a board game was *tæfl*, literally 'board', ultimately derived from the Latin *tabula*, probably via Scandinavian sources. But *tæfl* seems to have been a general term, much like the modern term 'cards', which denotes a family of games but not a specific version. The equivalent Anglo-Latin term was *alea*, which had originally meant a die (i.e. one of a pair of dice), but which had been transferred to indicate a board game with or without the use of dice. To complicate matters, one particular early medieval board game was known as *alea i.e. tabula*, meaning '*alea*, that is, the board game', or perhaps '*alea*, that is, the board game also known as *tabula*'. Finally, in traditional societies, where games come without a set of instructions written on the inside of the box, it is usual for games to develop different sets of rules in different times and periods, and so what went under a certain name across the culture may still have been played in a variety of ways.

The evidence suggests that the early English played a number of board games, all subsumed under the Old English term *tæfl*. A prominent example of these appears to have come from Scandinavia, where it became known as *hnefatafl*, 'the board game of the fist', the 'fist' being the central king piece. Although the term *hnefatafl* is Scandinavian rather than English, I will use it here for clarity. *Hnefatafl* was a game with varying numbers of pieces, but always in a 2:1 ratio, plus a king piece on one side.[259] So, for instance, one side might have four men plus a king piece; the other side might have eight men and no king piece. Sets might also be larger, for instance sixteen men versus eight men and a king, retaining the 2:1 ratio. Although few or no boards are known from England, boards of a size of 7 x 7, 9 x 9, and 11 x 11 squares or intersections have survived from Scandinavia, Scotland, and Ireland. The goal of the king's side was for the king to escape to the corners; the goal of the opposition was to capture the king. Despite the efforts of modern re-enactors, it is not certain how the pieces moved or how capture was effected. Two descriptions of the rules are known, one from a Welsh text of 1589 and one from the botanist Linnaeus in 1732, but neither is complete, and as the rules are usually reconstructed in the modern day, one side is favoured to win, which seems an unlikely imbalance for a game that remained popular over a wide region for hundreds of years.[260] Evidence that the Anglo-Saxons played the game comes from sets of game pieces that include a distinctive king piece and from the

---

[259] On *tæfl* and its meanings and background, see also Bayless, 'Alea, Tæfl, and Related Games'; Kimball, 'From Dróttin to King'; McLees, *The Games People Played;* Riddler, 'The Pursuit of Hnefatafl'; Hall, 'Board Games in Boat Burials'; and Gogosz, 'Chess and Hnefatafl'.
[260] Bayless, 'Alea, Tæfl, and Related Games'.

apperance of the definition *cyningstan on tæfle*, 'the king-piece in *tæfl*', in an eleventh-century glossary.[261] The king pieces found in England are abstract, though distinctively larger than accompanying pieces. In Scandinavia, some of the king pieces were fashioned as miniature figures sitting on chairs or thrones, sometimes holding their beard, perhaps as a sign of masculine power; and it has been proposed that the miniature figures may depict a god.[262] One king piece from Gloppen, Sogn og Fjordane, Norway makes the masculine aspect explicit in being vaguely phallic.[263] The game survived until at least 1889, when it was found to be still played among the Sámi, but since then this game, popular across north-west Europe for more than 1,000 years, is known only from revivals.[264]

At least some forms of *hnefatafl* were played without dice, but other sets of pieces, found both in England and elsewhere, include dice, and may indicate a variation of the game that included dice. In this, it resembled the second popular game of the period, *alea i.e. tabula*, a relative of modern backgammon, and descended, like backgammon, from the Roman board game *duodecim scripta*.[265] The game may have been known to Aldhelm in the seventh century: his treatise on metrics includes the phrase 'aleator calculis et tesseris ludens per aleam'[266] ('the *alea*-player playing *alea* with counters and dice'), although unfortunately this is in a discussion of metre and not of the game itself; but it is plausible to assume that this may refer to *alea i.e. tabula*. Although he was not an Englishman, the ninth-century Irishman Sedulius Scottus provided a possible second witness to the game when he discussed the double meaning of the term *alea* as 'die' and 'board game': 'a quodam ludo qui alea uocatur aleae dicuntur ubi sunt duae tabulae et multae tesserae'[267] ('*aleae* [dice] are so-called from a game which is called *alea*, where there are two boards and several dice'). The description of the two boards indicates that the game used a hinged board, like modern backgammon, which suggests that the game was *alea i.e. tabula*. The presence of the game is suggested by the survival of flat pieces, such as are used in modern backgammon; the pieces for the game need to be flat to

---

[261] The phrase is found translating the Latin *pirgus*, meaning a dice tower used in games requiring dice; the dice tower was probably equated to a king piece because both objects are taller than the regular pieces used in board games; Wright and Wülcker, *Anglo-Saxon and Old English Vocabularies*, vol. I, p. 151; Page, 'Old English *Cyningstan*'.

[262] Graham-Campbell, *Viking Artefacts,* nos. 99–101 and ills. 99–101; Roesdahl and Wilson, *From Viking to Crusader*, nos. 71, 77, and 123.

[263] The phallic piece (B 5150) is described by Solberg, 'Pastimes or Serious Business?', p. 267.

[264] The playing of the game in 1889 was described by Lindholm, *Hos Lappbönder*, p. 82.

[265] Schädler, 'XII Scripta, Alea, Tabula'.

[266] Aldhelm, *De pedum regulis*, in Ehwald, *Aldhelmi Opera*, cap. 120, p. 164.

[267] Löfstedt, *Grammatici Hibernici Carolini Aevi IV*, p. 94; compare Holtz, *Grammatici Hibernici Carolini Aevi I*, p. 69.

allow for the stacking which the game requires. This distinguishes the game from others such as the English *hnefatafl*, which typically has rounded pieces. The question is complicated by evidence of a hinged board for an unknown game played on a latticed board, in other words a game that was not *alea i.e. tabula*, found in three first-century burials from Britain.[268] This raises the possibility that hinged boards, such as Sedulius describes, may have belonged to yet another game; but, in any case, no hinged boards survive from the Anglo-Saxon period, and so the matter is purely speculative. The earliest surviving English *alea i.e. tabula* board is post-Conquest: this is the 'Gloucester tabula set', a board (now in fragments) and complete set of thirty spectacularly carved counters, excavated in Gloucester and possibly dating from as early as 1100.[269]

Other early medieval board games are known from surrounding cultures, but are harder to place definitively in England itself. The Roman game *ludus latrunculorum* or *latrunculi* (the term had the original meaning 'little soldiers') may well have survived into the early medieval period.[270] The game was played on a latticed board between two sides of equal number, and so sets of gaming pieces with equal numbers on each side, as are often excavated, may have belonged to this game. The Welsh, Irish, and Bretons also played a game between between two sides of equal number, which they called 'wood-sense': *gwyddbwyll* in Welsh, *gwezboell* in Breton, and *fidchell* in Irish. The name seems to have predated the division of languages, and so may be very ancient; or it is possible that 'wood-sense' is actually the same game as *latrunculi*. There is no clear evidence that this game was also played in England, but it would be unsurprising to find it there.

These games are all played on a latticed board, but later medieval England also saw a variety of board games of other kinds, played on a diagram of various shapes, including what are now called nine men's morris or merels, alquerque, and fox and geese. Some of these were unquestionably known in non-English regions in the earlier period: for instance, double-sided boards for *hnefatafl* and merels are known from the Gokstad ship burial, Toftanes on the Faroe Islands, and from Viking York.[271] A number of stone boards are also known from England, although most are probably post-Conquest; one exception may be the merels board found in Whitby.[272] Shorter and simpler than board games like *hnefatafl* or *alea i.e. tabula*, merels seems to have been an informal game played in snatched moments of

---

[268] Schädler, 'The Doctor's Game'.

[269] On this, see, for instance, Stewart and Watkins, 'An 11th-century Bone Tabula Set'.

[270] Schädler, 'Latrunculi'. On the early history of board games in Britain, see also Hall and Forsyth, 'Roman Rules?'.

[271] Moberly and Moberly, 'Nine Men's Medievalisms', p. 715.

[272] Hall, 'The Whitby Merels Board', gives a good survey of other medieval English merels boards; see also the extensive discussion in Moberly and Moberly, 'Nine Men's Medievalisms'.

idleness, and the boards are typically carved very roughly into the stone of monasteries, churches, stone buildings, and even of caves. Thus merels occupies a very different cultural and conceptual space from games like *hnefatafl*.

Although dice may have been used in some board games, there is also the possibility that dicing pure and simple was practised. In the Anglo-Saxon archaeological record, however, dice are much scarcer than gaming pieces. Two kinds of shaped dice are found, a square kind of the Roman type, surviving from the period ending around 650, and a slightly rectangular kind, characteristic of the tenth and eleventh centuries.[273] For whatever reason, few or no dice survive from the period between the eighth and the tenth centuries. One ancient and widespread form of dice is even less likely to be clear in the archaelogical record: animal knucklebones. The knucklebones of sheep, goats, and cattle have been employed as dice and in a variety of games worldwide.[274] Knucklebones have six distinct sides, and thus serve as dice without needing to be marked; indeed, modern six-sided dice are a direct descendent of knucklebones. Thus these can be used as dice for games that involve both dice and counters, such as *alea i.e. tabula*, or for pure dicing games; they were also widely used for divination. The use of dice or knucklebones for divination does not really qualify as a game, although it may have sometimes coloured gamers' approach to dice, particularly the sense that they were controlled by powers beyond the ken of the players.[275] Dicing games may have involved merely rolling the dice and hoping for or betting on certain results. Although dice games such as 'hazard' became wildly popular in the later medieval period, dicing is hard to trace at this early date, particularly as the term for a die, *alea*, was also used for board games so that it is hard to tell which is indicated when the term appears. Thus it is not clear which is meant when one hagiographer recounts how, in the time of Wulfstan, a cleric named Ælfsige 'solebat ... sub eadem arbore presertim aestiuis diebus aleis uel epulis uacare uel aliis ludis hilaritatem allicere' ('had the habit of spending leisure time under the tree, especially on a summer's day, dicing [*or* playing *tabula*?] or feasting, or indulging in some other kind of jollification').[276]

Another ancient game using knucklebones involved throwing them in the air and catching them on the back of the hand. This game, sometimes known as 'five-stones', was so widespread that it may well have been known in early

---

[273] Riddler and Trzaska-Nartowsk, 'Chanting upon a Dunghill'.

[274] For the uses of knucklebones in the ancient Mediterranean, see, for instance, Holmgren, '"Money on the Hoof"'.

[275] On the use of dice in divination, see Klingshirn, 'Defining the *Sortes Sanctorum*' and Chardonnens, *Anglo-Saxon Prognostics*.

[276] William of Malmesbury, *Saints' Lives*, pp. 94–95 (ii.17.2); my addition in sqaure brackets.

England; but knucklebones are typically not identifiable as playing pieces in the archaeological record, so the evidence is lacking.[277]

The premier board game of the later medieval period was chess, but it was apparently unknown to pre-Conquest England. The earliest evidence of chess in Britain comes not from England but from the Scottish Isle of Lewis, where the Lewis Chess set (dating probably from 1050–1070) had been imported from Norway.[278] In the post-Conquest period, chess was associated not merely with intellect but also with flirtation, an association that is absent from earlier medieval thought about board games.[279]

The importance of these games is indicated by the fact that game pieces are found widely in early Anglo-Saxon graves. Although the wooden boards have not survived, several thousand gaming pieces are known from fifth- through to seventh-century England, when they formed a standard part of grave goods.[280] The pieces surviving in grave goods were often made of bone, or sometimes of unshaped animal teeth; others were ceramic or glass, and elite sets could also be made of walrus ivory and whalebone. There is as yet no up-to-date comprehensive study of gaming pieces from early English graves, so a good deal remains to be explored.[281] It is clear, though, that gaming sets were common in high-status graves, and that the game was particularly associated with elite status. This is probably not an indication that such games were played only by the elite; the game pieces of ordinary people were doubtless made of wood (as indicated by the name of the Celtic game 'wood-sense') or even of pebbles, and these would not survive or show up in the archaeological record. Nevertheless, their presence in elite graves, and most particularly in the graves of rulers such as those buried at Taplow, Sutton Hoo, and Prittlewell, affirms that, as in the literary record, they were regarded as emblems of power and prestige, as certainly as the swords and feasting equipment that accompanied the gaming sets in those burials. It has been suggested that the martial and hierarchical aspects of games such as *hnefatafl* also helped inculcate boys into a culture of 'militarism and hegemonic masculinity'; but although boys must have observed board games, in the

---

[277] On games with knucklebones, see Hampe, *Die Stele aus Pharsalos*.

[278] Taylor, *The Lewis Chessmen*. Chess first appeared in Western Europe in the tenth century, where it had migrated from its origins in India.

[279] Murray, *A History of Chess*, pp. 434–37; Reeves, *Pleasures and Pastimes*.

[280] Riddler and Trzaska-Nartowsk, 'Chanting upon a Dunghill'.

[281] Some discussion of gaming pieces from graves is undertaken in, for example, Youngs, 'The Gaming-Pieces'; Riddler, Cameron, and Marzinzik, *Early Anglo-Saxon Personal Equipment*, pp. 5–7; Blackmore et al., *The Prittlewell Princely Burial*; and Stevens, 'On the Remains Found in an Anglo-Saxon Tumulus'.

archaeological and written records such games are overwhelmingly associated with adult life rather than with childhood.[282]

Practical issses of gender also remain to be investigated. Scandinavian burials indicate that at some times and places, board games were associated only with men; at other times and places, with both men and women.[283] The surviving written sources from England typically do not specify the identity of the player, but the few that do identify the player depict a man. This, again, may reflect the preponderance of men as the subject of literature rather than saying anything definitive about actual players of board games. Such games naturally operate in the symbolic realm, but even in *hnefatafl*, with its king and attackers, the symbolic was not always masculine. In the Old Norse *Hervarar saga ok Heiðreks* (*Saga of Hervor and Heidrek*), Odin takes part in a series of riddles, one of which characterises the game pieces as maidens attacking and defending their lord.[284]

Scandinavian literature also provides evidence of the ways in which board games were associated with gods and the supernatural; games and the supernatural are linked in multiple legends and sagas. Most prominently, the Old Norse *Voluspá* depicted the game of *tafl* played by the Æsir, the higher-order supernatural beings, at the creation, as if the game of *tafl* ordered the world. After Ragnarok, the destruction of the world, the *tafl* pieces will once more be found in the grass, as if waiting to be used to construct a new world.[285] With no written narratives of pagan religion surviving from pre-Christian England, such associations, if they existed, are irrecoverable, but the game did form the subject of an elaborate Christian allegory. The game in question was a complex version of *hnefatafl* called *alea euangelli*, 'the Board Game of the Gospel'. The colophon notes: 'Incipit alea euangelii quam Dubinsi episcopus Bennchorensis detulit a rege Anglorum, id est a domu Adalstani regis Anglorum'[286] ('Here begins the Board Game of the Gospel, which Dub Innse, bishop of Bangor, brought from the king of the English, that is, from the household of Athelstan, king of the English').

It is not clear whether it was merely the game that circulated at the court of Athelstan (924–939) or whether the allegory was circulating there as well. Unfortunately, the allegory itself is very dull, being a numerological treatise correlating the arrangement of the pieces on the board with canon tables. The

---

[282] Raffield, 'Playing Vikings'.

[283] On these aspects, see Bayless, 'Early Medieval Board Games'.

[284] Tolkien, *Saga Heiðreks Konungs*, no. 56, pp. 37–38.

[285] *Voluspá* 7–9 and 58, in Dronke, *The Poetic Edda*, vol. II, pp. 8–9.

[286] Robinson, *The Times of Saint Dunstan*, p. 173, with the diagram of the *alea* set-up reproduced as the frontispiece. A full-colour version is also available on the Digital Bodleian website (Corpus Christi College MS 122): http://image.ox.ac.uk/show?collection=corpus&manuscript=ms122. The diagram is on fol. 5v.

game itself, though, is elaborate to a degree unattested elsewhere in this early period. The board has 19 x 19 intersections, making it larger than any other board attested in Britain, and the playing pieces are divided according to the 2:1 ratio that puts the game in the *hnefatafl* family. The allegory specifies that the player must understand seven things: the 'duces ... ꝼ comites, propugnatores ꝼ impugnatores, ciuitatem et ciuitatulam, ꝼ .ix. gradibus bis'[287] ('dukes and counts, defenders and attackers, city and town, and in nine steps twice over'). It is not clear whether this roster refers to six different kinds of pieces or whether it refers to the two opponents: on one side, the dukes, who are the defenders of the city, and on the other, the counts, attackers from the town. In this regard, it may be relevant to note that such games often name the opposing sides after social or political forces; one Nordic variant of *tæfl*, for instance, called the two sides 'Swedes' and 'Muscovites'.[288] The 'nine steps twice over' may refer to the board, which has 18 x 18 squares, although the diagram in the manuscript specifies that the pieces themselves should be placed on the intersections of the lines, which are 19 x 19. There are fifty-four playing pieces, or perhaps fifty-eight, depicted in the manuscript diagram, and the placement of the pieces on the board appears very complicated, so much so that the scribe did not make the placement fully symmetrical, and his diagram is also at odds with some details of the textual description. All of this leads to the question whether the *alea evangelii* was actually ever played, or if it was only devised as a prop for the allegory. However disappointing the description of the game, it is clear that a board game was felt to be a worthy subject for religious allegory, and in that sense it bears continuity with earlier associations between board games and the supernatural principles of order.

Where games of skill suggested power and control, games with dice were associated with precariousness and the risks of fortune. This dimension appears in a tenth-century letter to Oswald, later included in the *Chronicle* of Ramsey Abbey, which uses the tumbling die as an image of the uncertainty of life, characterising life itself as a gamble: 'dum alealis tabulae tessera nutat'[289] ('while the die of the *alea* board tumbles'). Such comparisons were natural to dicing, and continued beyond the Norman Conquest: William of Malmesbury, for example, recounts the misfortunes of an early ruler of Britain in such a way: 'Inter haec tamen, quia fatalis alea incertis iactibus in huius uitae tabula mortales eludit, tantos bellorum euentus obfuscauit luctus domesticus'[290]

---

287 Robinson, *The Times of Saint Dunstan*, p. 173.

288 Payne, 'Did the Anglo-Saxons Play Games of Chance?', p. 330.

289 Macray, *Chronicon Abbatiae Rameseiensis*, p. 91.

290 William of Malmesbury, *Gesta Regum Anglorum*, vol. I, ed. and trans. Mynors, Thomson, and Winterbottom, p. 40 (Book I, ch. 17). The translation here is my own, since where others have regarded *tabula* as a dice table, I reserve the possibility that William is referring to the game of *tabula* which, like its descendent backgammon, uses dice.

(' But in the middle of these things, since in this board game of life the fatal die mocks mortals with its uncertain throws, a mournful event at home over-shadowed all these events of war').

Although the cultural position of board games persisted beyond the early medieval period, the coming of Christianity added tension to the equation. In some instances, such as that of the *alea euangelii*, the associations between board games and the greater order merely adapted to the new power structure. But although the secular elite continued to value the games, church authorities were dubious about whether games constituted a seemly occupation for clerics. Thus, religious texts expressed disapproval of gaming, classing it with other secular pursuits, albeit high-status secular pursuits. The eleventh-century *Canons of Edgar* warned that 'preost ne beo hunta ne hafecere ne tæflere' ('a priest should not be a hunter nor a hawker nor a player of board games').[291] Similarly, one of the *Vercelli Homilies* warned against 'idele spæca & tæflunga & gebeorscipas' ('frivolous speech and board games and drinking parties'), which were forbidden at all times, and most particularly on the Days of Rogation.[292] These admonitions serve as evidence that the official church frowned on games, but also as evidence that individual churchmen often did not.

Although the details of game play in Anglo-Saxon England remain frustrat-ingly elusive, evidence for the cultural position of games is stronger. Their frequency in grave goods and their position in literature suggest that games occupied the same role as they did in surrounding cultures: they were associated with the elite, with power and order, with skill and judgement – and with fun.

9 Conclusions: The Silent Hall

> Næs hearpan wyn,
> gomen gleobeames, ne god hafoc
> geond sæl swingeð, ne se swifta mearh
> burhstede beateð. Bealocwealm hafað
> fela feorhcynna forð onsended.
>   — *Beowulf* 2262–66

('There was no joy of the harp,
play of the glee-wood, nor does a good hawk
sail through the hall, nor does the swift steed
stamp in the stronghold. Baleful death has
sent forth the living.')

---

[291] Wulfstan, *Canons of Edgar*, p.14, no. 65 with parallel text on p. 15, no. 65.

[292] Homily for Monday in Rogationtide (no. XIX), in Scragg, *The Vercelli Homilies*, p. 320, lines 90–91.

In one sense, the world of the Anglo-Saxons is long gone: not only have their battles, struggles, politics, social world, and way of life long since disappeared, but their entertainments and amusements have faded to such an extent that even traces of them in the records are rare and fragmentary. In another sense, though, their practices live on. It is possible to see the seeds of later traditions in this early period, and to see inclinations and enjoyments that are not culturally specific but that typify human nature itself.

Although the Anglo-Saxons had numerous occasions on which they were enjoined to be serious – religious festivals, convocations, funerals – they often turned these into occasions of merrymaking. They relished challenges for the fun of it, whether in competition, such as horse racing, or in confronting peril, such as in boar-baiting. They took pleasure in display – particularly their own – as in the examples of nuns dressing as fine as brides or the showy rituals of the feast hall. They pursued their pleasures avidly whatever their means. The elite feasted elaborately and conspicuously on hard-to-obtain delicacies like leavened white bread and larks, paying for the poorer classes to supply the means for feasting and recreation and sometimes taxing them to compel them to supply these goods. But the poorer classes were no less determined to take their pleasures where they could, whether those were home-brewed feasts or game sets made out of wood and pebbles. Even lowly countrywomen crept away to the latrines and had their drinking parties where no one could stop them.

As a whole, then, it was a culture that revelled in communal merriment and enjoyed its pleasures out loud. They sang and danced; they relished music, storytelling, and sardonic humour. Their legends were lavishly filled with allusions to yet more legends, and they transmuted their history into stories. They mocked the hypocritical, versified even the most mundane of compositions, and delighted in paradoxes and riddles. They attempted to counterbalance the sombre aspects of existence, of which they were all too familiar, with enjoyment, both simple and sophisticated. Although their halls have long since fallen silent, while the Anglo-Saxons inhabited them, the halls, along with the rest of their world, were full of life.

References

Ælfric. *Ælfric's Lives of Saints*, ed. W. W. Skeat (4 vols.), vol. 2. London: Kegan Paul, Trench, Trübner and Co., 1900.

Ælfric. *Die Hirtenbriefe Ælfrics in Altenglischer und Lateinischer Fassung*, ed. B. Fehr (1914), repr. Darmstadt: Wissenschaftliche Buchgesellschaft, 1966.

Ælfric. *Ælfric's Catholic Homilies: The Second Series*, ed. M. R. Godden. Early English Text Society, s. s. 5. Oxford: Oxford University Press, 1979.

Ælfric. *Ælfric's Catholic Homilies: The First Series – Text*, ed. P. Clemoes. Early English Text Society s. s. 17. Oxford: Oxford University Press, 1997.

Ælfric. *Ælfric's Catholic Homilies: Series I and II – Commentary*, ed. M. R. Godden. Early English Text Society, s. s. 18. Oxford: Oxford University Press, 2000.

Ælfric Bata. *Anglo-Saxon Conversations: The Colloquies of Ælfric Bata*, ed. S. Gwara, trans. with Introduction by D. W. Porter. Woodbridge: Boydell, 1997, pp. 59–204.

Aldhelm. *De pedum regulis*. In R. Ehwald (ed.), *Aldhelmi Opera*. Monumenta Germaniae Historica, Auctores Antiquissimi XV. Berlin: Weidmann, 1919.

Aldhelm. *Aldhelm: The Prose Works*, trans. M. Lapidge and M. Herren. Ipswich: D. S. Brewer, 1979.

Aldhelm. *Aldhelmi Malmesbiriensis Prosa de virginitate cum glosa latina atque anglosaxonica*, ed. S. Gwara. Corpus Christianorum Series Latina 124. Turnhout: Brepols, 2001.

Anlezark, D. *The Old English Dialogues of Solomon and Saturn*. Cambridge: Boydell and Brewer, 2009.

Arngart, O. 'The Durham Proverbs'. *Speculum* 56:2 (1981), 288–300.

Asser. *Asser's Life of King Alfred*, ed. W. H. Stevenson. Oxford: Clarendon Press, 1957.

Aubrey, J. *Remaines of Gentilisme and Judaisme*, ed. J. Britten. London: W. Satchell, Peyton, and Co., 1881.

Barillari, S. M. 'Le maschere cornute nella tradizione europea (storia, onomastica, morfologia)'. In D. Porporato and G. Fassino (eds.), *Sentieri della memoria*. Bra: Slow Food Editore, 2015, pp. 529–48.

Barlow, F. *Edward the Confessor*. London: Eyre and Spottiswood, 1970.

Barlow, F. (ed. and trans.). *The Life of King Edward Who Rests at Westminster, Attributed to a Monk of St. Bertin*, 2nd ed. Oxford: Clarendon Press, 1992.

Battles, P. and C. D. Wright. '*Eall-feala Ealde Sæge*: Poetic Performance and "The Scop's Repertoire" in Old English Verse'. *Oral Tradition* 32:1 (2018), 3–26.

Bayless, M. 'Alcuin's *Disputatio Pippini* and the Early Medieval Riddle Tradition'. In G. Halsall (ed.), *Humour, History and Politics in Late Antiquity and the Early Middle Ages*. Cambridge: Cambridge University Press, 2001, pp. 157–78.

Bayless, M. 'Humour and the Comic in Anglo-Saxon England'. In S. Hordis and P. Hardwick (eds.), *English Medieval Comedy*. Turnhout: Brepols, 2007, pp. 13–30.

Bayless, M. 'Alea, Tæfl, and Related Games: Vocabulary and Context'. In K. O'B. O'Keeffe and A. Orchard (eds.), *Latin Learning and English Lore*, 2 vols. Toronto: University of Toronto Press, 2015, vol. 2, pp. 9–27.

Bayless, M. 'The Fuller Brooch and Anglo-Saxon Depictions of Dance'. *Anglo-Saxon England* 45 (2016), 183–212.

Bayless, M. 'Merriment, Entertainment, and Community in Anglo-Saxon Culture'. In C. Biggam, C. Hough, and D. Izdebska (eds.), *The Daily Lives of the Anglo-Saxons*. Tempe, AZ: Arizona Center for Medieval and Renaissance Studies, 2017, pp. 239–56.

Bayless, M. 'Early Medieval Board Games: Issues of Power and Gender'. In M. Bayless, J. Lillequist, and L. Webb (eds.), *Gender and Status Competition in Pre-Modern Culture*. Turnhout: Brepols. 2021, pp. 185–207.

Bazire, J. and J. E. Cross (eds.). *Eleven Old English Rogationtide Homilies*. Toronto: University of Toronto Press, 1982.

Bede. *Venerabilis Baedae Opera Historica*, ed. C. Plummer, 2 vols. Oxford: Clarendon Press, 1896.

Bede. *Bede's Ecclesiastical History of the English People*, ed. B. Colgrave and R. A. B. Mynors. Oxford: Oxford University Press, 1969.

Bede. *De temporum ratione liber*, ed. C. W. Jones. Corpus Christianorum Series Latina 123B. Turnhout: Brepols, 1977.

Bede. *Ecclesiastical History of the English People*, trans. Leo Sherley-Price, rev. R. E. Latham. London: Penguin, 1990.

Bedingfield, M. B. *The Dramatic Liturgy of Anglo-Saxon England*. Woodbridge: Boydell, 2002.

Benko, S. E. 'Anglo-Saxon Musical Instruments'. Unpublished PhD dissertation, State University of New York at Stony Brook, 1983. https://bit.ly/3JbSCNZ.

Biddle, M. (ed.). *Winchester in the Early Middle Ages: An Edition and Discussion of the Winton Domesday*. Oxford: Clarendon Press, 1976.

Biddle, M. *Object and Economy in Medieval Winchester*, 2 vols. Winchester Studies 7. Oxford: Oxford University Press, 1990.

Billington, S. 'The Midsummer Solstice as It Was, or Was Not, Observed in Pagan Germany, Scandinavia, and Anglo-Saxon England'. *Folklore* 119:1 (2008), 41–57.

Binchy, D. A. (ed.). *Corpus iuris Hibernici*, 7 vols. Dublin: Dublin Institute for Advanced Studies, 1978.

Birch, W. de G. (ed.). *Cartularium Saxonicum*, 3 vols. London: Whiting and Co., 1885–1899.

Bitterli, D. *Say What I Am Called: The Old English Riddles of the Exeter Book and the Anglo-Latin Riddle Tradition*. Toronto: University of Toronto Press, 2009.

Blackmore, L., I. Blair, S. Hirst, and C. Scull. *The Prittlewell Princely Burial: Excavations at Priory Crescent, Southend-on-Sea, Essex, 2003*. London: Museum of London Archaeology, 2019.

Boenig, R. 'The Anglo-Saxon Harp'. *Speculum* 71 (1996), 290–320.

Boethius, A. M. S. *Anicii Manlii Torquati Severini Boetii De institutione arithmetica libri duo, De institutione musica libri quinque*, ed. G. Friedlein. Leipzig: Teubner, 1867.

Boethius, A. M. S. *Fundamentals of Music*, trans. C. M. Bower, ed. C. V. Palisca. New Haven, CT: Yale University Press, 1989.

Bredehoft, T. A. 'OE *Yðhengest* and an Unrecognized Passage of Old English Verse'. *Notes and Queries* 54:2 (2007), 120–22.

Breeze, S. 'The Status of Secular Musicians in Early Medieval England: Ethnomusicology and Anglo-Saxon Musical Culture'. *Mediaevalia* 42 (2021), 1–39.

Bremmer R. H., Jr. 'The Germanic Context of "Cynewulf and Cyneheard" Revisited'. *Neophilologus* 81 (1997), 445–65.

Britnell, R. H. *The Commercialisation of English Society, 1000–1500*. Cambridge: Cambridge University Press, 1993.

Brown, Marjorie A. 'The Feast Hall in Anglo-Saxon Society'. In M. Carlin and J. T. Rosenthal, (eds.), *Food and Eating in Early Medieval Europe*. London: Hambleton Press, 1998, pp. 1–14.

Bruce-Mitford, R. L. S. *The Sutton Hoo Ship Burial*, 3 vols. London: British Museum Press, 1975–1983.

Buckland, T. 'The Reindeer Antlers of the Abbots Bromley Horn Dance: A Re-examination'. *Lore and Language* 3 (1980), 1–8.

Bullough, D. A. *Friends, Neighbours and Fellow-drinkers: Aspects of Community and Conflict in the Early Medieval West*. H. M. Chadwick Memorial Lecture 1. Cambridge: Department of Anglo-Saxon, Norse, and Celtic, 1990.

Butterfield, A. 'Vernacular Poetry and Music'. In Mark Everist (ed.), *The Cambridge Companion to Medieval Music*. Cambridge: Cambridge University Press, 2011, pp. 205–24.

Byrhtferth of Ramsay. *Byrhtferth of Ramsay: The Lives of St Oswald and St Ecgwine*, ed. M. Lapidge. Oxford: Oxford University Press, 2009.

Caldwell, J. (ed.). *The Oxford History of English Music*. Oxford: Clarendon Press, 1999.

Cesario, M. 'The Shining of the Sun in the Twelve Nights of Christmas'. In S. McWilliams (ed.), *Saints and Scholars: New Perspectives on Anglo-Saxon Literature and Culture in Honour of Hugh Magennis*. Woodbridge: Boydell and Brewer, 2012, pp. 195–212.

Chandler, C. J. 'Charlemagne's Table: The Carolingian Royal Court and Food Culture'. *Viator* 50:1 (2019), 1–30.

Chardonnens, L. S. *Anglo-Saxon Prognostics, 900–1100: Study and Texts*. Leiden: Brill, 2007.

Clark, C. *Words, Names, and History: Selected Writings of Cecily Clark*, ed. P. Jackson. Cambridge: D. S. Brewer, 1995.

Clayton, M. 'An Edition of Ælfric's *Letter to Brother Edward*'. In E. Treharne and S. Rosser (eds.), *Early Medieval English Texts and Interpretations: Studies Presented to Donald G. Scragg*. Tempe, AZ: Arizona Center for Medieval and Renaissance Studies, 2002, pp. 262–83.

Colgrave, B. (ed. and trans.). *Two Lives of St Cuthbert*. Cambridge: Cambridge University Press, 1985.

Colker, M. L. 'Texts of Jocelyn of Canterbury Which Relate to the History of Barking Abbey'. *Studia Monastica* 7:2 (1965), 383–460.

Colman, F. *The Grammar of Names in Anglo-Saxon England*. Oxford: Oxford University Press, 2014.

Crawford, S. *Childhood in Anglo-Saxon England*. Stroud: Sutton, 1999.

Crawford, S. 'Children, Grave Goods and Social Status in Early Anglo-Saxon England'. In Joanna Sofaer Derevenski, (eds.), *Children and Material Culture*. London: Routledge, 2000, pp. 169–79.

Cross, J. E. and Thomas D. Hill (eds. and trans.). *The* Prose Solomon and Saturn *and* Adrian and Ritheus. Toronto: University of Toronto Press, 1982.

Cubbin, G. P. *The Anglo-Saxon Chronicle: A Collaborative Edition*. Vol. 6: MS. D. Woodbridge: D. S. Brewer, 1996.

Cubitt, C. 'Folklore and Historiography: Oral Stories and the Writing of Anglo-Saxon History'. In E. M. Tyler and R. Balzaretti (eds.), *Narrative and History in the Early Medieval West*. Turnhout: Brepols, 2006, pp. 189–223.

Davidson, C. 'Erotic "Women's Songs" in Anglo-Saxon England'. *Neophilologus* 59 (1975), 451–62.

De Vegvar, C. N. 'Beyond Valkyries: Drinking Horns in Anglo-Saxon Women's Graves'. In C. E. Kozikowski and H. Scheck (eds.), *New Readings on Women and Early Medieval English Literature and Culture: Cross-Disciplinary*

Studies in Honour of Helen Damico. Leeds: Arc Humanities Press, 2019, pp. 43–60.

Dick, E. S. 'Æ. *dream*: zur Semantik der Verbalbeziehungen in der Dichtung'. In K. R. Jankowsky and E. S. Dick (eds.), *Festschrift für Karl Schneider*. Amsterdam: John Benjamins, 1982, pp. 121–35.

Diller, H.-J. 'Joy and Mirth in Middle English (and a Little Bit in Old): A Plea for the Consideration of Genre in Historical Semantics'. In J. Fisiak and A. Kiełkiewicz-Janoviak, (eds.) *Middle English Miscellany: From Vocabulary to Linguistic Variation*. Poznań: Motivex, 1996, pp. 83–105.

Dobbie, E. V. K. (ed.). *The Anglo-Saxon Minor Poems*. Anglo-Saxon Poetic Records 6. London: Routledge & Kegan Paul, 1942.

Dobney K. and D. Jaques. 'Avian Signatures for Identity and Status in Anglo-Saxon England'. *Acta Zoologica Cracoviensia* 45 (2002), 7–21.

Doyle, C. 'Beer and Ale in Early Medieval England: A Survey of Evidence'. In J. A. Geck, R. O'Neill, and N. Phillips (eds.), *Beer and Brewing in Medieval Culture and Contemporary Medievalism*. Cham: Palgrave Macmillan, 2022, pp. 33–56.

Dronke, U. (ed. and trans.). *The Poetic Edda*, vol. II: *Mythological Poems*. Oxford: Clarendon Press, 1997.

Dümmler, E. (ed.). *Epistolae Karolini Aevi II*. Monumenta Germaniae Historica Epistolae IV. Berlin: Weidmann, 1895.

Düwel, K. *Runenkunde*. Stuttgart: Metzler, 1968.

Eadmer. *Eadmer of Canterbury: Lives and Miracles of Saints Oda, Dunstan, and Oswald*, ed. A. J. Turner and B. J. Muir. Oxford Medieval Texts. Oxford: Clarendon Press, 2006.

Earl, J. W. 'Beowulf's Rowing-Match'. *Neophilologus* 63:2 (1979), 285–90.

Eddius Stephanus. *The Life of Bishop Wilfrid by Eddius Stephanus*, ed. B. Colgrave. Cambridge: Cambridge University Press, 1927.

Enright, M. J. *Lady with a Mead Cup: Ritual, Prophecy, and Lordship in the European Warband from La Tène to the Viking Age*. Blackrock, Ireland: Four Courts Press, 1996.

Evans, A. C. *The Sutton Hoo Ship Burial*, rev. ed. London: British Museum Press, 1994.

Evison, V. I. *An Anglo-Saxon Cemetery at Great Chesterford, Essex*. Council for British Archaeology Report 91. York: CBA, 1994.

Fabiszak, M. *The Concept of 'Joy' in Old and Middle English: A Semantic Analysis*. Pila: Wyzsza Szkola Biznesu, 2001/2002.

Fahey, R. 'The Wonders of Ebrietas: Drinking and Drunkenness in Old English and Anglo-Latin Riddles'. In J. A. Geck, R. O'Neill, and N. Phillips (eds.),

Beer and Brewing in Medieval Culture and Contemporary Medievalism. Cham: Palgrave Macmillan, 2022, pp. 315–39.

Felix. *Felix's Life of St Guthlac*, ed. and trans. B. Colgrave. Cambridge: Cambridge University Press, 1985.

Fell, F. 'Old English *Beor*'. *Leeds Studies in English* n.s. 8 (1975), 76–95.

Filotas, B. *Pagan Survivals, Superstitions and Popular Cultures in Early Medieval Pastoral Literature.* Toronto: Pontifical Institute of Mediaeval Studies, 2005.

Fleming, R. 'The New Wealth, The New Rich and the Political Style in Late Anglo-Saxon England'. *Anglo-Norman Studies* 23 (2001), 1–22.

Fletcher, A. J. 'Jugglers Celtic and Anglo-Saxon'. *Theatre Notebook* 44 (1990), 1–10.

Flight, T. 'Aristocratic Deer Hunting in Late Anglo-Saxon England: A Reconsideration, Based Upon the *Vita S. Dunstani*'. *Anglo-Saxon England* 45 (2016), 311–31.

Frank, R. 'The Search for the Anglo-Saxon Oral Poet'. *Bulletin of the John Rylands Library* 75:1 (1993), 11–36.

Frazer, J. G. *Spirits of the Corn and of the Wild.* 2 vols. London: Macmillan, 1912 (vol. 7 of *The Golden Bough*, 3rd ed.).

Gaimar, Geffrei. *Estoire des Engleis: History of the English*, ed. Ian Short. Oxford: Oxford University Press, 2009.

Gale, D. A. 'The Seax'. In S. C. Hawes (ed.), *Weapons and Warfare in Anglo-Saxon England.* Oxford: Oxford University Press, 1989, pp. 71–84.

Gautier, A. *Le festin dans l'Angleterre anglo-saxonne.* Rennes: Presse Universitaire de Rennes, 2006.

Gautier, A. 'Cooking and Cuisine in Late Anglo-Saxon England'. *Anglo-Saxon England* 41 (2013), 373–406.

Gelling, M. 'Some Meanings of "Stow"'. In S. Pearce (ed.), *The Early Church in Britain and Ireland.* Oxford: BAR, 1982, pp. 187–96.

Geoffrey of Monmouth. *The Historia Regum Britannie of Geoffrey of Monmouth*, ed. N. Wright. 1: Bern, Bürgerbibliothek, MS. 568. Cambridge: D. S. Brewer, 1985.

Gerald of Wales. *De Rebus a se Gestis.* Vol. 1 of *Giraldi Cambrensis Opera*, ed. J. S. Brewer, G. F. Warner, and J. F. Dimock (8 vols.). London: Longman, Green, Longman, and Roberts, 1861–1891.

Gerald of Wales. *The Autobiography of Giraldus Cambrensis*, trans. H. E. Butler. London: Jonathan Cape, 1937.

Gerald of Wales. *Speculum Ecclesiae.* Vol. 4 of *Giraldi Cambrensis Opera*, ed. J. S. Brewer, G. F. Warner, and J. F. Dimock (8 vols.). Cambridge: Cambridge University Press, 2012.

Girvan, R. (ed.). *Ratis Raving*. Scottish Text Society, 3rd series 11. Edinburgh: William Blackwood and Sons, 1939.

Godden, M. 'New Year's Day in Late Anglo-Saxon England'. *Notes and Queries* 237, n.s. 39:2 (1992), 148–50.

Gogosz, R. '"Hver er sterkastr?" The Sports and Games of the Northmen in the Middle Ages. Role, Rules and Aspects: Study with the Special Focus on Saga-Age Iceland'. Unpublished PhD dissertation, University of Rzeszów, 2016. https://bit.ly/3QgRCfo. Accessed 23 April 2024.

Gogosz, R. 'Chess and Hnefatafl: Playing Board Games in Old Icelandic Literature'. In A. Stempin (ed.), *The Cultural Role of Chess in Medieval and Modern Times*. Poznań: Muzeum Archeologiczne w Poznaniu, 2018, pp. 207–18.

Gómez, M. and F. Javier. 'Mixing Pleasure and Beauty: Positive Aesthetic Experience in Old English Poetry'. *Journal of English Studies* 18 (2020), 153–79.

Goolden, P. *The Old English* Apollonius of Tyre. Oxford: Oxford University Press, 1958.

Goossens, L. *The Old English Glosses of MS. Brussels, Royal Library 1650*. Brussels: der Academiën, 1974.

Graham-Campbell, J. *Viking Artefacts: A Select Catalogue*. London: British Museum Publications, 1980.

Greene, R. L. *The Early English Carols*. 2nd ed. Oxford: Oxford University Press, 2019.

Guðmundsson, F. (ed.). *Orkneyinga saga*. Reykjavík: Hid Íslenzka Fornritafélag, 1965.

Haddan, A. W. and W. Stubbs (eds.). *Councils and Ecclesiastical Documents Relating to Great Britain and Ireland*. 3 vols. Oxford: Clarendon Press, 1869–1878.

Hagen, A. *A Second Handbook of Anglo-Saxon Food and Drink: Production and Distribution*. Hockwold cum Norton, Norfolk: Anglo-Saxon Books, 1995.

Hall, M. A. 'The Whitby Merels Board'. *Yorkshire Archaeological Journal* 77 (2005), 25–29.

Hall, M. A. 'Board Games in Boat Burials: Play in the Performance of Migration and Viking Age Mortuary Practice'. *European Journal of Archaeology* 19:3 (2016), 439–55.

Hall, M. A. and K. Forsyth. 'Roman Rules? The Introduction of Board Games to Britain and Ireland'. *Antiquity* 85:330 (2015), 1325–38.

Hammon, A. 'The Brown Bear'. In T. O'Connor and N. Sykes (eds.), *Extinctions and Invasions: A Social History of British Fauna*. Oxford: Windgather Press, 2010, 95–103.

Hampe, R. *Die Stele aus Pharsalos im Louvre.* Berlin: W. de Gruyter, 1951.

Harbus, Antonina. 'Joy in the Emotional Life of the Anglo-Saxons'. In C. Biggam, C. Hough, and D. Izdebska (eds.), *The Daily Lives of the Anglo-Saxons.* Tempe, AZ: Arizona Center for Medieval and Renaissance Studies, 2017, pp. 187–203.

Harmer, F. E. '*Chipping* and *Market*: A Lexicographical Investigation'. In C. Fox and B. Dickins (eds.), *The Early Cultures of North-West Europe.* Cambridge: Cambridge University Press, 1950, pp. 333–60.

Harper, E. 'Toys and the Portable Antiquities Scheme: A Source for Exploring Later Medieval Childhood in England and Wales'. *Childhood in the Past* 11:2 (2018), 85–99.

Harrison, K. 'The Beginning of the Year in England, c. 500–900'. *Anglo-Saxon England* 2 (1973), 51–70.

Hawkes, S. C., H. R. Ellis Davidson, and C. Hawkes. 'The Finglesham Man'. *Antiquity* 39 (1965), 17–34.

Haydon, F. S. (ed.). *Eulogium (historiarum sive temporis): Chronicon.* 3 vols. London: Longman, Brown, Green, Longmans, and Roberts, 1858–1863.

Heinemann, F. J. '"Cynewulf and Cyneheard" and *Landnámabók*'. *Leeds Studies in English* n.s. 24 (1993), 57–89.

Hill, T. D. '"When the Leader is Brave … ": An Old English Proverb and its Vernacular Context'. *Anglia* 119:2 (2001), 232–36.

Holmgren, R. '"Money on the Hoof": The Astragalus Bone – Religion, Gaming and Primitive Money'. In B. S. Frizell (ed.), *PECUS: Man and Animal in Antiquity.* Rome: Swedish Institute in Rome, 2004, pp. 212–20.

Holtz, L. (ed.). *Grammatici Hibernici Carolini Aevi I.* Corpus Christianorum Series Latina 40. Turnhout: Brepols, 1977.

Hooke, D. *The Landscape of Anglo-Saxon England.* Leicester: Leicester University Press, 1998.

Hope-Taylor, B. *Yeavering: An Anglo-British Centre of Early Northumbria.* London: Her Majesty's Stationery Office, 1977 (repr. London: British Heritage, 2009).

Hutton, R. *The Stations of the Sun: A History of the Ritual Year in Britain.* Oxford: Oxford University Press, 1996.

Irvine, S. *The Anglo-Saxon Chronicle: 7. MS E.* Cambridge: Boydell and Brewer, 2004.

Irvine, S. and M. R. Godden (ed. and trans.) *The Old English Boethius with Verse Prologues and Epilogues Associated with King Alfred.* 2 vols. Cambridge, MA: Harvard University Press, 2012.

Jolly, K. 'Prayers from the Field: Practical Protection and Demonic Defense in Anglo-Saxon England'. *Traditio* 61 (2006), 95–147.

Jurasinski, S. and L. Oliver. *The Laws of Alfred: the* Domboc *and the Making of Anglo-Saxon Law*. Cambridge: Cambridge University Press, 2021.

Kelly, F. *Early Irish Farming: A Study Based Mainly on the Law-Texts of the 7th and 8th Centuries*. Dublin: Dublin Institute for Advanced Studies, 1997.

Keynes, S. and M. Lapidge (trans.). *Alfred the Great: Asser's Life of King Alfred and Other Contemporary Sources*. New York: Penguin, 2004.

Kimball, J. J. L. 'From Dróttin to King: The Role of Hnefatafl as a Descriptor of Late Iron Age Scandinavian Culture'. *Lund Archaeological Review* 19 (2013), 61–76.

Kindschi, L. 'The Latin-Old English Glossaries in Plantin-Moretus MS. 32 and British Museum MS. Additional 32246'. Unpublished PhD dissertation, Stanford University, 1955.

Klingshirn, W. E. 'Defining the *Sortes Sanctorum*: Gibbon, Du Cange, and Early Christian Lot Divination'. *Journal of Early Christian Studies* 10:1 (2002), 77–130.

Konshuh, C. '*Anraed* in their *Unraed*: The Æthelredian Annals (983–1016) and their Presentation of Kings and Advisors'. *English Studies* 97:2 (2016), 140–62.

Kramer, J. *Between Heaven and Earth: Liminality and the Ascension of Christ in Anglo-Saxon Literature*. Manchester: Manchester University Press, 2014.

Krapp, G. P. and E. V. K. Dobbie (eds.). *The Exeter Book*. Anglo-Saxon Poetic Records 3. New York: Columbia University Press, 1963.

Lambert, T. and S. Leggett. 'Food and Power in Early Medieval England: Rethinking *Feorm*'. *Anglo-Saxon England* 49 (2022), 107–53.

Lapidge, M. (ed.). *The Cult of St Swithun*. Oxford: Clarendon Press, 2003.

Leach, E. E. 'Music and Masculinity in the Middle Ages'. In I. Biddle and K. Gibson (eds.), *Masculinity and Western Musical Practice*. Farnham: Ashgate, 2009, pp. 21–40.

Lee, C. *Feasting the Dead: Food and Drink in Anglo-Saxon Burial Rituals*. Woodbridge: Boydell, 2007.

Lester, G. A. 'The Cædmon Story and its Analogues'. *Neophilologus* 58 (1974), 225–37.

Lewis, C. 'Children's Play in the Later Medieval English Countryside'. *Childhood in the Past* 2:1 (2009), 86–108.

Lewis, F. 'Gwerin Ffristial a Thawlbwrdd'. *Transactions of the Honourable Society of Cymmrodorion* (1941), 185–205.

Liebermann, F (ed.). *Die Gesetze der Angelsachsen*. 3 vols. Halle: Max Niemeyer, 1898–1916.

Lilliard, R. 'The Deer Parks of Domesday Book'. *Landscape* 4:1 (2003), 4–23.

Lindenbaum, S. 'Entertainment in English Monasteries'. In J.C. Aubailly (ed.), *Le Théatre et la cité dans l'Europe médiévale*. Stuttgart: Akademischer Verlag, 1988. (Also *Fifteenth Century Studies* 13 (1988), 411–34.)

Lindholm, P. A. *Hos Lappbönder*. Stockholm: Albert Bonnier, 1884.

Liuzza, R. M. (ed. and trans.). *Anglo-Saxon Prognostics: An Edition and Translation of Texts from London, British Library, MS Cotton Tiberius A. iii*. Cambridge: D. S. Brewer, 2011.

Löfstedt, B. (ed.). *Grammatici Hibernici Carolini Aevi IV*. Corpus Christianorum Series Latina 40 C. Turnhout: Brepols, 1977.

MacGregor, A. *Bone, Antler, Ivory and Horn: The Technology of Skeletal Materials since the Roman Period*. London: Croom Helm, 1985.

MacGregor, A., A. J. Mainman, and N. S. H. Rogers (eds.). *Craft, Industry, and Everyday Life: Bone, Antler, Ivory and Horn from Anglo-Scandinavian and Medieval York* (The Archaeology of York, ed. P. V. Addyman, vol. 17, fasc.12: *The Small Finds*). York: Council for British Archaeology (for the York Archaeological Trust), 1999.

Macray, W. D. (ed.). *Chronicon Abbatiae Rameseiensis*. London: Longman, 1886.

Magennis, H. 'The *Beowulf* Poet and his "druncne dryhtguman"'. *Neuphilologische Mitteilungen* 86:2 (1985), 159–64.

Magennis, H. 'Images of Laughter in Old English Poetry, with Particular Reference to the "Hleahtor Wera" of the Seafarer'. *English Studies* 73:3 (1992), 193–204.

Magennis, H. *Images of Community in Old English Poetry*. Cambridge: Cambridge University Press, 1996.

Magennis, H. *Anglo-Saxon Appetites: Food and Drink and Their Consumption in Old English and Related Literature*. Dublin: Four Courts Press, 1999.

Magnusson, M. and H. Palsson (trans.). *Njals Saga*. Harmondsworth: Penguin, 1996.

Map, Walter. *De nugis curialium: Courtiers' Trifles*, ed. and trans. M. R. Jame s, C. N. L. Brooke, and R. A. B. Mynors. Oxford: Oxford University Press, 1983.

Marsden, R. *The Cambridge Old English Reader*, 2nd ed. Cambridge: Cambridge University Press, 2015.

Martin, J. D. 'Sports and Games in Icelandic Saga Literature'. *Scandinavian Studies* 75 (2003), 27–32.

Marvin, W. P. *Hunting Law and Ritual in Medieval English Literature*. Cambridge: D. S. Brewer, 2006.

McGuire, E. '"Whim Rules the Child": The Archaeology of Childhood in Scandinavian Scotland'. *Journal of the North Atlantic* 11 (2019), 13–27.

McLees, C. *The Games People Played: Gaming Pieces, Boards, and Dice from Excavations in the Medieval Town of Trondheim, Norway.* Trondheim: Fortiden i Trondheim Bygrunn, 1990.

McNeill, J. T. and H. M. Gamer. *Medieval Handbooks of Penance.* New York: Columbia University Press, 1938.

McNeill, W. H. *Keeping Together in Time: Dance and Drill in Human History.* Cambridge, MA: Harvard University Press, 1997.

McTurk, R. W. '"Cynewulf and Cyneheard" and the Icelandic Sagas'. *Leeds Studies in English* n.s. 12 (1981), 81–127.

Meaney, A. L. *A Gazetteer of Early Anglo-Saxon Burial Sites.* London: Allen & Unwin, 1964.

Mees, B. 'Batavian *Pero* and Germanic **pero* "pear"'. *Amsterdamer Beiträge zur älteren Germanistik* 82:1 (2022), 1–14.

Meritt, H. D. *The Old English Prudentius Glosses at Boulogne-sur-Mer.* Stanford, CA: Stanford University Press, 1955.

Moberly, K. and B. Moberly. 'Nine Men's Medievalisms: *Conquests of the Longbow*, Nine Men's Morris, and the Impossibilities of a Half-Forgotten Game's Ludic Past'. In A. Classen (ed.), *Pleasure and Leisure in the Middle Ages and Early Modern Age.* Berlin: W. de Gruyter, 2019, pp. 695–722.

Muir, B. J. (ed.). *The Exeter Anthology of Old English Poetry*, 2nd ed. 2 vols. Exeter: University of Exeter Press, 2004.

Mullally, R. *The Carole: A Study of a Medieval Dance.* Farnham: Ashgate, 2011.

Murray, H. J. R. *A History of Chess.* London: Oxford University Press, 1913.

Napier, A. S. (ed.). *The Old English Version of the Enlarged Rule of Chrodegang.* Early English Text Society, o.s. 150. London: Kegan Paul, Trench, Trübner & Co., 1916.

Ng, E. 'Swinging the Top: A Crux in the Old English *Apollonius of Tyre*'. Paper delivered at the Fourth ASSC Graduate Student Conference, Yale University, 16 February 2008. www.eching.org/wp-content/uploads/2008_apolloniu s_yale.pdf (revised version of the conference paper).

Niles, J. D. *Homo Narrans: The Poetics and Anthropology of Oral Literature.* Philadelphia, PA: University of Pennsylvania Press, 1999 (also available as 'Reconceiving *Beowulf*: Poetry as Social Praxis', *College English* 61:2 (1998), 143–66).

Niles, J. D. 'The Myth of the Anglo-Saxon Poet'. *Western Folklore* 62:1/2 (2003), 7–61.

Niles, J. D. 'Bede's Cædmon: "The Man Who Had No Story" (Irish Tale-Type 2412B)'. *Folklore* 117 (2006), 141–55.

Oggins, R. S. *The Kings and Their Hawks: Falconry in Medieval England*. New Haven, CT: Yale University Press, 2004.

Ogilvy, J. D. A. '*Mimi, Scurrae, Histriones*: Entertainers of the Early Middle Ages'. *Speculum* 38:4 (1963), 603–19.

O'Keeffe, K. O'B. *Visible Song: Transitional Literacy in Old English Verse*. Cambridge: Cambridge University Press, 1990.

Opland, J. *Anglo-Saxon Oral Poetry: A Study of the Traditions*. New Haven, CT: Yale University Press, 1980.

O'Rahilly, C. (trans.). *Táin Bó Cúalnge from the Book of Leinster*. Dublin: Dublin Institute of Advanced Studies, 1970. https://celt.ucc.ie/published/T301035.html. Accessed 24 April 2024.

Orchard, A. (ed. and trans.). *The Old English and Anglo-Latin Riddle Tradition*. Dumbarton Oaks Medieval Library 69. Cambridge, MA: Harvard University Press, 2021.

O'Regan, H. J. 'The Presence of the Brown Bear *Ursus arctos* in Holocene Britain: A Review of the Evidence'. *Mammal Review* 48:4 (2018), 229–44.

Orme, N. *Medieval Children*. New Haven, CT: Yale University Press, 2001.

Page, C. 'Anglo-Saxon *Hearpan*: Their Terminology, Technique, Tuning and Repertory of Verse, 850–1066'. Unpublished PhD dissertation, University of York, 1981.

Page, C. 'The Carol in Anglo-Saxon Canterbury?' In E. Hornby and D. Maw (eds.), *Essays on the History of English Music in Honour of John Caldwell: Sources, Style, Performance, Historiography*. Woodbridge: Boydell, 2010, pp. 259–69.

Page, R. 'Old English *Cyningstan*'. *Leeds Studies in English* n.s. 3 (1969), 1–5.

Pálsson, H. and P. Edwards (trans.). *Orkneyinga Saga: The History of the Earls of Orkney*. London: Penguin, 1978.

Parker, E. *Winters in the World: A Journey through the Anglo-Saxon Year*. London: Reaktion, 2022.

Pasternak, C. B. *The Textuality of Old English Poetry*. Cambridge: Cambridge University Press, 1995.

Payne, I. 'Did the Anglo-Saxons Play Games of Chance? Some Thoughts on Old English Board Games'. *Antiquaries Journal* 86 (2006), 330–45.

Paz, J. *Nonhuman Voices in Anglo-Saxon Literatuure and Material Culture*. Manchester: Manchester University Press, 2017.

Pertz, G. H. (ed.). *Capitularia regum Francorum*. Monumenta Germaniae Historica III, *Leges* I. Hanover: Hahn, 1835.

Petersen, N. H. 'Les textes polyvalents du *Quem quaeritis* à Winchester au Xe siècle'. *Revue de musicologie* 86:1 (2000), 105–18.

Pollington, S. 'The Mead-Hall Community'. *Journal of Medieval History* 37:1 (2011), 19–33.

Porter, D. W. 'The Anglo-Latin Elegy of Herbert and Wulfgar'. *Anglo-Saxon England* 40 (2011), 225–47.

Powell, H. '"Once Upon a Time There Was a Saint . . .": Re-evaluating Folklore in Anglo-Latin Hagiography'. *Folklore* 121:2 (2010), 171–89.

Price, J. 'Theatrical Vocabulary in Old English: A Preliminary Survey (1)'. *Medieval English Theatre* 5 (1983), 58–71.

Price, J. 'Theatrical Vocabulary in Old English (2)'. *Medieval English Theatre* 6 (1984), 101–25.

Raffield, B. 'Playing Vikings: Militarism, Hegemonic Masculinities, and Childhood Enculturation in Viking Age Scandinavia'. *Current Anthropology* 60:6 (2019), 813–35.

Rauer, C. (ed. and trans.). *The Old English Martyrology*. Cambridge: D. S. Brewer, 2013.

Reeves, C. *Pleasures and Pastimes in Medieval England*. Stroud: Sutton, 1995.

Rice, M. A. *Abbots Bromley*. Shrewsbury: Wilding and Son, 1939.

Riddler, I. D. 'The Pursuit of Hnefatafl'. In Irving Finkel (ed.), *Ancient Board Games in Perspective*. London: British Museum Press, 2006, pp. 349–54.

Riddler, I. and N. Trzaska-Nartowsk. 'Chanting upon a Dunghill: Working Skeletal Materials in Anglo-Saxon England'. In M. C. Hyer, G. R. Owen-Crocker, and C. P. Biggam (eds.), *The Material Culture of Daily Living in the Anglo-Saxon World*. Exeter: University of Exeter Press, 2011, pp. 116–41.

Riddler, I., E. Cameron, and S. Marzinzik. *Early Anglo-Saxon Personal Equipment and Structural Ironwork from Saltwood Tunnel, Kent*. CTRL Specialist Report Series. York: Archaeology Data Service, 2006.

Roberts, J. M., M. J. Arth, and R. R. Bush. 'Games in Culture'. *American Anthropologist* 61:4 (1959), 597–605.

Robertson, A. J. (ed.). *Anglo-Saxon Charters*, 2nd ed. Cambridge: Cambridge University Press, 1956.

Robinson, F. C. 'Notes and Emendations to Old English Poetic Texts'. *Neuphilologische Mitteilungen* 67:4 (1966), 356–64.

Robinson, J. A. *The Times of Saint Dunstan*. Oxford: Clarendon Press, 1923.

Roesdahl E. and D. M. Wilson (eds.). *From Viking to Crusader*. New York: Rizzoli, 1992.

Roud, S. *The English Year*. London: Penguin, 2006.

Russom, G. R. 'A Germanic Concept of Nobility in *The Gifts of Men* and *Beowulf*'. *Speculum* 53:1 (1978), 1–15.

Sawyer, P. H. *Anglo-Saxon Charters: An Annotated List and Bibliography*. London: Royal Historical Society, 1968.

Sawyer, P. H. 'Early Fairs and Markets in England and Scandinavia'. In B. L. Anderson and A. J. H. Latham (eds.), *The Market in History*. London: Routledge, 1986, pp. 59–77.

Schädler, U. 'Latrunculi – ein verlorenes strategisches Brettspiel der Römer'. In G. G. Bauer (ed.), *Homo Ludens: Der spielende Mensch IV*. Munich: Emil Katzbichler, 1994, pp. 47–67.

Schädler, U. 'XII Scripta, Alea, Tabula – New Evidence for the Roman History of "Backgammon"'. In A. J. de Voogt (ed.), *New Approaches to Board Game Research*. Leiden: IIAS, 1995, pp. 73–98.

Schädler, U. 'The Doctor's Game – New Light on the History of Ancient Board Games'. In P. Crummy (ed.), *Stanway: An Elite Burial Site at Camulodunum*. London: Society for the Promotion of Roman Studies, 2007, pp. 359–75.

Schneider, K. *Die germanischen Runennamen*. Meisenheim: A. Hain, 1956.

Scragg, D. G. (ed.). *The Vercelli Homilies and Related Texts*. Early English Text Society 300. Oxford: Oxford University Press, 1992.

Solberg, B. 'Pastimes or Serious Business? Norwegian Graves with Gaming Objects *c*. 200–1000 AD'. In B. Hardh, K. Jennberht, and D. Olaussonm (eds.), *On the Road: Studies in Honour of Lars Larsson*. Stockholm: Almqvist and Wiksell, 2007, pp. 265–69.

Stevens, J. 'On the Remains Found in an Anglo-Saxon Tumulus at Taplow, Buckinghamshire'. *Journal of the British Archaeological Association* 40 (1884), 61–71.

Stewart, I. and M. Watkins. 'An 11th-century Bone Tabula Set from Gloucester [Preliminary Account]'. *Medieval Archaeology* 28 (1984), 185–90.

Stokes, P. A. 'The Vision of Leofric: Manuscript, Text and Context'. *Review of English Studies* n.s. 63:261 (2011), 529–50.

Sveinsson, E. Ó (ed.). *Brennu-Njáls saga*. Íslenzk fornrit 12. Reykjavík: Hið íslenzka bókmenntafélag, 1954.

Swanton, M. *Three Lives of the Last Englishmen*. New York: Garland, 1984.

Sykes, N. 'Deer, Land, Knives and Halls: Social Change in Early Medieval England'. *Antiquaries Journal* 90 (2010), 175–93.

Sykes, N. 'Woods and the Wild'. In H. Hamerow, D. A. Hinton, and S. Crawford (eds.), *The Oxford Handbook of Anglo-Saxon Archaeology*. Oxford: Oxford University Press, 2011, pp. 327–45.

Symons, T. (ed.). *Regularis Concordia Anglicae Nationis Monachorum Sanctimonialiumque*. (*The Monastic Agreement of the Monks and Nuns of the English Nation*). London: Nelson, 1953.

Taylor, M. *The Lewis Chessmen*. London: British Museum Publications, 1978.

Tengvik, G. *Old English Bynames*. Uppsala: Almqvist & Wiksells Boktryckeri-a.-b.,1938.

Thornbury, E. *Becoming a Poet in Anglo-Saxon England*. Cambridge: Cambridge University Press, 2016.

Thorpe, B. *Ancient Laws and Institutes of England*. 2 vols. London, 1840 (repr. Cambridge: Cambridge University Press, 2012).

Tolkien, C. (ed. and trans.). *Saga Heiðreks Konungs ins Vitra: The Saga of King Heidrek the Wise*. London: Thomas Nelson and Sons, 1960.

Tolley, C. (ed. and trans.). *Gróttasongr: The Song of Grotti*. London: Viking Society for Northern Research, 2008.

Trafford, S. 'Swimming in Anglo-Saxon England'. In C. Twomey and D. Anlezark (eds.), *Meanings of Water in Early Medieval England*. Turnhout: Brepols, 2021, pp. 85–107.

Tucker, S. I. 'Laughter in Old English Literature'. *Neophilologus* 43 (1959), 222–26.

Tupper, F. Jr. 'Anglo-Saxon Dæg-Mæl'. *PMLA* 10:2 (1895), 111–241.

Tydeman, W. (ed.). *The Medieval European Stage, 500–1500*. Cambridge: Cambridge University Press, 2001.

Van Arsdall, A. *Medieval Herbal Remedies: The Old English Herbarium and Anglo-Saxon Medicine*. New York: Taylor & Francis, 2002.

Wace. *Le Roman de Rou de Wace*, ed. A. J. Holden, vol. 2. Paris: Picard, 1970.

Wallis, R. J. '"As the Falcon Her Bells" at Sutton Hoo? Falconry in Early Anglo-Saxon England'. *Archaeological Journal* 174:2 (2017), 409–36.

Walsh, M. W. 'Medieval English Martinmesse: The Archaeology of a Forgotten Festival'. *Folklore* 111:2 (2000), 231–54.

Webster, L. 'The Prittlewell (Essex) Burial: A Comparison with Other Anglo-Saxon Princely Graves'. In T. A. S. M. Panhuysen (ed.), *Transformations in North-Western Europe (AD 300–1000)*. Stuttgart: Theiss, 2011, pp. 266–72.

Weiskott, E. *English Alliterative Verse: Poetic Tradition and Literary History*. Cambridge: Cambridge University Press, 2016.

Whitelock, D. (ed. and trans.). *Anglo-Saxon Wills*. Cambridge: Cambridge University Press, 1930.

Wilcox, J. (ed.). *Humour in Anglo-Saxon Literature*. Cambridge: Boydell, 2000.

Wilcox, J. 'Understatement and Incongruity: Humour in the Literature of Anglo-Saxon England'. In V. Westbrook and S.-l. Chao (eds.), *Humour in the Arts: New Perspectives*. New York: Routledge, 2018, pp. 59–77.

Wilcox, J. *Humour in Old English Literature: Communities of Laughter in Early Medieval England*. Toronto: University of Toronto Press, 2023.

William of Malmesbury. *Gesta Regum Anglorum*, 2 vols., ed. R. A. B. Mynors, completed by R. M. Thompson and M. Winterbottom. Oxford: Clarendon Press, 1998–1999.

William of Malmesbury. *Saints' Lives: Lives of SS. Wulfstan, Dunstan, Patrick, Benignus and Indract*, ed. M. Winterbottom and R. M. Thomson. Oxford: Clarendon Press, 2002.

William of Malmesbury. *Gesta Pontificum Anglorum*, ed. M. Winterbottom with R. M. Thomson. 2 vols. Oxford: Clarendon Press, 2007.

William of Malmesbury. *Gesta Pontificum Anglorum: The History of the English Bishops, Vol. 1: Text and Translation*, ed. M. Winterbottom. Oxford Scholarly Editions Online, 2019. https://bit.ly/44ocbfZ. Accessed 3 May 2024.

Williams A. and G. H. Martin (trans.). *Domesday Book: A Complete Translation*. London: Penguin, 1992.

Wilmart, A. 'La légende de Ste Édithe en prose et vers par le moine Goscelin'. *Analecta Bollandiana* 56 (1938), 265–307.

Winterbottom, M. 'An Edition of Faricius, *Vita S. Aldhelmi*'. *Journal of Medieval Latin* 15 (2005), 93–147.

Winterbottom, M. and M. Lapidge (eds. and trans.). *The Early Lives of St Dunstan*. Oxford Medieval Texts. Oxford: Oxford University Press, 2012.

Wrenn, C. L. 'A Saga of the Anglo-Saxons'. *History* 25 (1940), 208–15.

Wright, C. W. *The Cultivation of Saga in Anglo-Saxon England*. Edinburgh: Oliver and Boyd, 1939.

Wright, T. *A History of Domestic Manners and Sentiments in England during the Middle Ages*. London: Chapman & Hall, 1892.

Wright, T. and R. P. Wülcker. *Anglo-Saxon and Old English Vocabularies*. 2 vols. Darmstadt: Wissenschaftlche Buchgesellscaft, 1968.

Wulfstan. *The Homilies of Wulfstan*, ed. D. Bethurum. Oxford: Clarendon Press, 1957.

Wulfstan. *Wulfstan's Canons of Edgar*, ed. R. Fowler. Early English Text Society 266. London: Oxford University Press, 1972.

Wulfstan. *Sermo Lupi ad Anglos*, ed. D. Whitelock, rev. ed. Exeter: Exeter University Press, 1976.

Wulfstan of Winchester. *The Life of St Æthelwold*, ed. and trans. M. Lapidge and M. Winterbottom. Oxford Medieval Texts. Oxford: Oxford University Press, 1991.

Youngs, S. M. 'The Gaming-Pieces'. In R. Bruce-Mitford (ed.), *The Sutton Hoo Ship-Burial* (3 vols.), vol. 3, part 2, ed. A. Care Evans. London: British Museum Publications, 1983, pp. 853–74.

Ziolkowski, J. (ed. and trans.). *The Cambridge Songs (Carmina cantabrigiensia)*. New York: Garland, 1994.

Ziolkowski, J. 'Nota Bene: Why the Classics Were Neumed in the Middle Ages'. *Journal of Medieval Latin* 10 (2000), 74–114.

Ziolkowski, J. M. 'Women's Lament and the Neuming of the Classics'. In J. Haines and R. Rosenfeld (eds.), *Music and Medieval Manuscripts: Paleography and Performance*. Burlington, VT: Ashgate, 2004, pp. 128–50.

Cambridge Elements ☰

England in the Early Medieval World

Megan Cavell
University of Birmingham
Megan Cavell is Associate Professor in Medieval English Literature at the University of Birmingham. She works on a wide range of topics in medieval literary studies, from Old and early Middle English and Latin languages and literature to riddling, gender and animal studies. Her previous publications include *Weaving Words and Binding Bodies: The Poetics of Human Experience in Old English Literature* (2016), *Riddles at Work in the Early Medieval Tradition: Words, Ideas, Interactions* (co-edited with Jennifer Neville, 2020), and *The Medieval Bestiary in England: Texts and Translations of the Old and Middle English Physiologus* (2022)

Rory Naismith
University of Cambridge
Rory Naismith is Professor of Early Medieval English History in the Department of Anglo-Saxon, Norse and Celtic at the University of Cambridge, and a Fellow of Corpus Christi College, Cambridge. Also a Fellow of the Royal Historical Society, he is the author of *Early Medieval Britain 500–1000* (Cambridge University Press, 2021), *Citadel of the Saxons: The Rise of Early London* (2018), *Medieval European Coinage, with a Catalogue of the Coins in the Fitzwilliam Museum, Cambridge, 8: Britain and Ireland c. 400–1066* (Cambridge University Press, 2017) and *Money and Power in Anglo-Saxon England: The Southern English Kingdoms 757–865* (Cambridge University Press, 2012, which won the 2013 International Society of Anglo-Saxonists First Book Prize).

Winfried Rudolf
University of Göttingen
Winfried Rudolf is Chair of Medieval English Language and Literature in the University of Göttingen (Germany). Recent publications include *Childhood and Adolescence in Anglo-Saxon Literary Culture* (with Susan E. Irvine, 2018). He has published widely on homiletic literature in early England and is currently principal investigator of the ERC-Project ECHOE–Electronic Corpus of Anonymous Homilies in Old English.

Emily V. Thornbury
Yale University
Emily V. Thornbury is Associate Professor of English at Yale University. She studies the literature and art of early England, with a particular emphasis on English and Latin poetry. Her publications include *Becoming a Poet in Anglo-Saxon England* (Cambridge, 2014), and, co-edited with Rebecca Stephenson, *Latinity and Identity in Anglo-Saxon Literature* (2016). She is currently working on a monograph called *The Virtue of Ornament*, about pre-Conquest theories of aesthetic value.

About the Series
Elements in England in the Early Medieval World takes an innovative, interdisciplinary view of the culture, history, literature, archaeology and legacy of England between the fifth and eleventh centuries. Individual contributions question and situate key themes, and thereby bring new perspectives to the heritage of early medieval England. They draw on texts in Latin and Old English as well as material culture to paint a vivid picture of the period. Relevant not only to students and scholars working in medieval studies, these volumes explore the rich intellectual, methodological and comparative value that the dynamic researchers interested in England between the fifth and eleventh centuries have to offer in a modern, global context. The series is driven by a commitment to inclusive and critical scholarship, and to the view that early medieval studies have a part to play in many fields of academic research, as well as constituting a vibrant and self-contained area of research in its own right.

Cambridge Elements ≡

England in the Early Medieval World

Elements in the Series

Crime and Punishment in Anglo-Saxon England
Andrew Rabin

Europe and the Anglo-Saxons
Francesca Tinti

Art and the Formation of Early Medieval England
Catherine E. Karkov

Writing the World in Early Medieval England
Nicole Guenther Discenza, Heide Estes

Multilingualism in Early Medieval Britain
Lindy Brady

Recovering Old English
Kees Dekker

Entertainment, Pleasure, and Meaning in Early England
Martha Bayless

A full series listing is available at: www.cambridge.org/EASW